THE DURABLE USE OF CONSUMER PRODUCTS:
New Options for Business and Consumption

THE DURABLE USE OF CONSUMER PRODUCTS:
New Options for Business and Consumption

Edited by

MICHEL KOSTECKI

University of Neuchâtel

KLUWER ACADEMIC PUBLISHERS
DORDRECHT / BOSTON / LONDON

A C.I.P Catalogue record for this book is available from the Library of Congress.

658.562
D947

ISBN 0-7923-8145-9

Published by Kluwer Academic Publishers,
P.O. Box 17, 3300 AA Dordrecht, The Netherlands

Sold and distributed in North, Central and South America
by Kluwer Academic Publishers,
P.O. Box 358, Accord Station, Hingham, MA 02018-0358, U.S.A.

In all other countries, sold and distributed
by Kluwer Academic Publishers, Distribution Center,
P.O. Box 322, 3300 AH Dordrecht, The Netherlands

ab

Printed on acid-free paper

Printed and bound in Great Britain

"For me, an object is alive. This cigarette, this match box contain a secret life much more intensive than certain human beings".

Joan Miró (Taillandier, Yvon (1959) XXe siècle, Paris).

TABLE OF CONTENTS

Part II. Cases and Business Perspectives

PREFACE

Do we need a new car or a new refrigerator every ten years? What happens to our PC which is exchanged for a new model every three years? Why do our shoes last only a year or so, while those of our great grandfather served for a generation? Are businesses deliberately marketing products in a way which encourages sub-optimal use and induces consumers to buy new products?

More and more consumers respond "yes" objecting to the business practices which reduce the life span of a product or pay no attention to efficiency in consumption. The growing concern with sub-optimal use of consumer durables arises as a response to the volume of waste, as well as to the growing conviction that over-consumption is encouraged by marketing techniques and approaches that favor lesser durability and sub-optimal use.

There are signs that those things will have to change.

Firstly, client orientation – a condition *sine qua non* of marketing success in the saturated markets of rich countries – is gaining popularity. Consumers are better informed and more influential and "intelligent consumption" is on the rise. Buyers are becoming more and more hostile towards marketing manipulation, inducing them to consume faster, more and at higher prices. The public increasingly resists messages in advertisements (preventive resistance) which are predominantly persuasive (rather than educational or informative) and conceived to stimulate demand for the "new", the superficial and the fashionable. A growing number of users is also critical of consumer goods which become too complex to be repaired, used optimally or rendered compatible with systems based on newer technologies or fashions.

Secondly, innovative managers view the evolution of the marketing environment as a window of business opportunities. Indeed, a growing group of business leaders look at the "optimal use" option as a realistic profit-making proposition. The contributors of this collective book – authorities in the area of sustainable product design, waste management and marketing of services – argue that greater emphasis should be put on durable use of consumer products if marketing concepts such as client orientation, product stewardship or sustainable consumption are to be effectively applied in business. Case studies of leading firms such as Rank Xerox, Kodak, Daimler-Benz and Digital are included in this volume to illustrate how longer life spans of consumer products may bring about reduction in waste, greater market share, increased customer loyalty and higher profits.

ix

Product durability strategies are gaining importance because they:
- emphasize performance and maximize client satisfaction rather than quantitative consumption;
- protect the environment through less waste and through more intensive use;
- open new opportunities to service clients and integrate specific products into more comprehensive service-based systems providing solutions to clients' problems;
- intensify the partnership between producers and their customers focusing on confidence, interaction and mutual commitment.

Strategies aiming at the durable use of consumer products necessarily involve producers, consumers and governments. Consumer durables, in order to be optimally used, require appropriate communication strategies, systems of retake and re-marketing, maintenance services, etc.. Marketing – the art of exchanges – is a key element of such activities.

This volume is a first book-length analysis of the durable use of consumer products from a marketing perspective. It offers a fresh look at a number of conceptual issues such as:
- What are the reasons for the shorter life of products?
- What are the functional, economic and symbolic attributes of product durability?
- How do those attributes relate to the consumer's utilitarian, cognitive and affective motives of buying?
- What methods of communication show the advantages of durability to the consumer (and when does it make sense to use them)?
- What are the managerial concerns in the area of retake and re-marketing?
- What management knowledge and marketing techniques still need to be developed to operate an optimal system for the usage of consumer durables?

Several authors of this volume challenge companies to seek radical improvements in the way in which they develop their product concept and think about product utilization by customers. They pull together hard-headed arguments for innovative companies to force the pace of optimal use.

The volume is divided into two parts. Part I, entitled "Concepts and Issues", offers an overview of the theoretical issues . It also provides an outline of the various approaches and methodologies used. Part II, titled "Cases and Business Perspectives", comprises the "practical" chapters presenting cases and specific business solutions.

Part I begins with an overview of the durability issue from the marketing perspective and an outline of the approaches and methodologies that are helpful in conceptualizing the optimal use of durables (Chapter 1). Following that, is a comparative analysis of a service economy and industrial economy (Chapter 2) giving the reader a better understanding of the environmental change affecting the use of products. Chapter 2 concludes with a series of strategic implications for consumer marketing.

The relationship between marketing strategies and the useful life of products is more explicitly discussed in Chapter 3, which also provides an overview of the challenges facing managers. The concepts of product stewardship and extended product responsibility are presented in Chapter 4. Chapter 5 deals with sustainable design and Chapter 6 draws lessons from the experiences of the US electronics industry.

Chapters by practitioners comprised in Part II provide a wealth of hands-on advice on how to move towards a goal seen as too elusive for many businesses to bother about. Which sectors seem to be the most likely candidates for change? How does one find out whether the rising trend towards the optimal use of products has implications for a particular company? A useful tool for checking a company's attitude is the questionnaire (Annex 1) providing a benchmark from which managers may identify their company's current position and assess profitable opportunities.

We hope that this volume will assist managers, strategic planners, academics and government specialists. We also dare to expect that the book will be of interest to the public at large since the issues discussed are those confronted by many people in their day-to-day life.

M. M. Kostecki   Neuchâtel, January 1998

LIST OF TABLES AND FIGURES

Tables

Figures

ACKNOWLEDGEMENTS

We could not have written this book without the outstanding help and encouragement of many people. In producing this volume, we wish to recognize and show our appreciation to the sponsors of this project: The Swiss National Science Foundation, the Swiss Club of Marketing and the University of Neuchâtel.

Our gratitude is also to the city of Neuchâtel for making the Palais du Peyrou available to us, the authors of this book, to exchange views on early drafts. The volume is partly based on the papers presented at the *Fourth Neuchâtel Conference on Marketing Strategies* organized by the Enterprise Institute in Neuchâtel (Switzerland) in the summer of 1996. The participants of this conference included some of the world's foremost authorities on sustainable product design, product stewardship and marketing of services. We are particularly grateful for their comments and suggestions.

Thanks to our editor, Mrs. Pamela Schaffner, who made our writing look better than it really is, and helped us polish the final draft of this manuscript.

Lastly, I would like to express my warmest thanks to my assistants Mr. Philippe Burki, Mr. Maarten de Groot, Miss Patrizia Ventimiglia, and to my secretary Mrs. Yvette Fischer for their contribution, which was both willing and efficient. However, no one mentioned is responsible for the views expressed in this volume or for any inaccuracies. That responsibility is ours alone.

Michel Kostecki   Neuchâtel, January 1998

CONTRIBUTORS

The Editor:
MICHEL KOSTECKI is Director of The Enterprise Institute and professor of marketing at the University of Neuchâtel, Switzerland. During the Uruguay Round, he was the Counselor at the GATT in Geneva. Dr. Kostecki was a professor of economics and international business at the Ecole des Hautes Etudes Commercials (HEC) of the University of Montreal (1976–1982) and a research associate at Harvard Business School. His recent volumes include: *Service Economies in Eastern Europe* (edited with A. Fehervary), Oxford, Pergamon Press, 1996, *The Political Economy of the World Trading System*, Oxford University Press, 1995 (with B. Hoekman), and *Marketing Strategies for Services*, Oxford, Pergamon Press, 1994.

EWA BOGACKA-KISIEL is professor of management and finance at the Academy of Economics in Wroclaw (Poland). She has published extensively on finance-related issues and marketing of services and serves as a consultant to banks and other financial institutions in Eastern and Central Europe.

MARTIN CHARTER is a manager and consultant specializing in "business and environment" issues. His is a Joint Coordinator of the Center for Sustainable Design and Coordinator of SHEBA (Surrey & Hampshire Environmental Business Association) in the UK. Dr. Charter is a director of Eco-Innovations Publishing (an imprint of Epsilon Press Ltd.) specializing in the electronic publication of "business and environment" books and information, the Chief in Editor of "The Green Management Letter" and the European Editor of *The Journal of Corporate Environmental Strategy*. He has published books and articles on green business issues.

PATRICIA S. DILLON is a research associate at the Gordon Institute of Tufts University, Massachusetts, United States, where she specializes in environment-related business strategy and policy studies. Dr. Dillon has recently finalized an important research project, commissioned by the US Administration, dealing with the managerial and economic issues of environmental protection in the electronic industry. For the past several years, Dr. Dillon has also provided consultation on several projects of the World Business Council for Sustainable Development (WBCSD).

MAARTEN DE GROOT AND BRYN MCCROSSAN MAIRE are research assistants at the Enterprise Institute of the University of Neuchâtel, Switzerland. Mr de Groot graduated in Psychology and Mrs McCrossan Maire in Management Science at the same University.

WIKTOR KISIEL is, at the time of writing, a research associate at the Faculty of Mathematics and Physics of the University of Wroclaw (Poland). He holds a Ph.D. in physics from the same university and serves as a consultant on "technology and environment" to private businesses, governments and international organizations.

IRINA MASLENNIKOVA is Environmental Manager for Rank Xerox Ltd. where she is closely associated with the development of the company's product stewardship program across the world. Dr. Maslennikowa holds a Ph.D. in Environmental Protection from Lomonosov University in Moscow and has several years of international business experience.

RICHARD MERLOT, Corporate Program Manager, Digital Equipment Corporation, is responsible for the implementation of the product stewardship program throughout Digital Europe. He joined Digital in 1984 and has held a number of senior management positions including Strategic planning for technology at Digital Ayr, Scotland. Mr. Merlot holds an Engineering degree from the Ecole Nationale Supérieure d'Arts & Métiers (Paris) and a certificate in Business Management from the Ecole Supérieure de Commerce & d'Administration des Entreprises (Lyon).

WALTER R. STAHEL is Director of The Product-Life Institute, Geneva, Switzerland. He is the author of pioneering studies and books in the field of service economies and durable use of products and acts as consultant to major international organizations, governments and companies in his area of expertise. His previous assignments included research work at the Battelle Institute and at the International Association for Insurance Economics Research, known as the Geneva Association. Mr. Stahel is co-author of the Club of Rome study on "The Limits to Certainty" (with Orio Giarini). He holds an engineering degree (architecture) from the Swiss Federal Institute of Technology (ETH) in Zurich, and is a Mitchell Prize Laureate (1982).

HANS H. VAN TEFFELEN is Manager, Environmental Affairs Europe, Africa & Middle Eastern Region at the Eastman Kodak Company (Netherlands). His current responsibilities include the development and the implementation of Kodak's environment-friendly strategies based on re-manufacturing and product conversions. Mr Teffelen has more than 20 years of managerial experience in international business firms and has conducted numerous environment-related projects world-wide.

JAN-OLAF WILLUMS is Director of the World Business Council for Sustainable Development (WBCSD) – a coalition of 120 international companies united by a shared commitment to the principles of sustainable development. He is also professor at the Norwegian School of Management in Oslo. Dr. Willums has extensive experience in management and consulting. He holds a Ph.D. in Engineering from the Massachusetts Institute of Technology (MIT) and a Masters degree from the Swiss Federal Institute of Technology (ETH) in Zurich. His recent volumes include: *From Ideas to Action: Business and Sustainable Development* (1992) (with U. Golüke).

CHAPTER 1

MARKETING AND DURABLE USE OF CONSUMER PRODUCTS:
A Framework for Inquiry

MICHEL KOSTECKI

Director, The Enterprise Institute, University of Neuchâtel

"Consumption may be regarded as a vast pit-fall, situated on the high road of life, which we have no sense enough of our common interest to agree to fill up, or fence round, heedless fathers and mothers are for ever guiding their sons and daughters directly into it". (Thomas Beddoos, 1832)

The life span of numerous consumer durables has declined over the last decades and product life cycles continue to shrink in product categories such as household equipment, cars, personal computers and clothing. Should the consumer durable have a longer life? What is the consumer's attitude towards product durability and how does it affect his buying decision? How do the leading firms practicing customer-orientation and waste prevention respond to the new concerns related to use of products? What innovative marketing techniques and approaches might be adopted to optimize the durable use of products to the benefit of consumers, producers and society at large? This chapter suggests that the durable use of products provides a window of opportunities for innovative firms and that marketing and "durability services" around products remain central to this new orientation.

1. OPTIMAL USE AND CONSUMER DURABLES

There are three ways to become satisfied: (1) to desire less, (2) improve consumption of what is already available, and (3) to acquire more and more material goods. It is the latter option that binds together the industrial countries where material culture continues to dominate and where it is nourished by the constant flow of commodities.

One of the underlying assumptions of this study is that the traditional *modus operandi* of the mass consumption economies is breaking down. First, the meas-

1

M. Kostecki (ed.) The Durable Use of Consumer Products, 1–28.
© 1998 *Kluwer Academic Publishers. Printed in Great Britain.*

urement of performance in terms of output growth is met with criticism and there is an increase in support for evaluating economic success in terms of indicators referring to quality of life, environmental performance, and quality of human relations.

Second, the attitudes towards consumption and production are changing. On the one hand, production and consumption are interdependent as consumers are increasingly encouraged to contribute to the production process (e.g. self-service and partnership in problem solving). Consequently, utility is often created through a joint effort between producers and consumers. It is more and more difficult to draw a line between the producer's output and the consumer's "production" of satisfaction in the consumption process. On the other hand, the boarders between production and consumption are also blurred because consumption sometimes means "hard work" and production (work) frequently provides a source of satisfaction.

Finally, client orientation is categorically imperative for a successful performance in the modern economy (Vandermerwe, 1994). It signifies that not only production but also product utilization should remain at the center of a producer's concerns. An effective client-oriented strategy means that the producer's performance is evaluated in terms of his contribution to the client's value chain and that optimal use of products is an issue of interest both to the suppliers and to the users.

Product life (or durability) is the product's actual life in use. It may be different to *the product's economic life* which is determined by the opportunity cost. The product's economic life takes into account the total cost of product utilization in comparison to the cost of using new products. It may be shorter than the *product's technical life* which is determined by the duration of a product's ability to fulfill its technical function.

A lot may be learned from experience with producer goods. There are several reasons why industrial durables (machines, equipment) are used more efficiently than consumer durables. First, the buying process and use are less "rational" and professional in the case of consumer durables than producer durables. Second, symbolic content is, *in ceteris paribus,* more important for consumer goods than for producer goods. This creates a scope for consumer manipulation (see proposition 4 below) and a risk that a product which is viable from the technical, functional and economic view is considered obsolete due to its symbolic attributes.

The optimal use of consumer durables is a neglected aspect of the modern economy. This has to change because product use is an important component of productivity. Traditionally, productivity increases are thought to result from investments, labor quality, or better organization. However, improved productivity in use may also increase ability to satisfy human needs with given resources. Consequently, the concept of efficiency should also comprise "client-oriented" dimensions such as client participation in production, improved client use of products as well as the perceived value of the client (Table 1.1).

Table 1.1

HOW TO INCREASE PRODUCTIVITY?
CLASSIC APPROACH INVESTMENTS QUALITY OF LABOR ORGANISATION
FAVOUR CLIENT PARTICIPATION IN PRODUCTION AND IN MARKETING
IMPROVE CLIENT'S USE OF PRODUCTS
OPTIMISE PERCEIVED VALUE OF PRODUCTS

A synergy between the producer and his client provides an interesting option for partnership in production. Innovative approaches aimed at enhancing services largely consist of redistributing certain activities between the chain of activities of the supplier and the chain of activities of the client (Levitt, 1981).

Box 1

Producer-client Synergy: The Case of IKEA
The traditional chain of activities of a manufacturer/distributor of furniture such as IKEA involves: 1. furniture design, 2. production of components, 3. assembly of components, 4. packaging and labeling, 5. transportation and storage, 6. promotion & sale and 7. customer services (e.g. delivery and maintenance service). The client chain of activities traditionally comprises (a) information search, (b) transportation to the shop & parking, (c) visiting the shop while taking care of children, (d) making the choice, (e) purchasing, (f) taking delivery of the furniture and (g) placing the furniture piece in an appropriate place at home. Substantial synergies do exist for the cooperation between suppliers and their clients at various stages of their respective chains of activities. IKEA – an international producer and distributor of furniture – intervenes at stage (c) of the client's chain of activities by taking care of the client's children. In exchange, it encourages the consumer to contribute at stage 3 and 7 of the production chain. New information technologies create numerous new options for synergies of that nature e.g. for greater client involvement at stage 1.

The optimal use of products has three interrelated dimensions: (i) consumer's efficiency, (ii) intensive use (i.e., consumption of a product by a large number of consumers) and (iii) durable use (i.e., an optimal life of a product).

Table 1.2

DIMENSIONS OF OPTIMAL USE OF PRODUCTS
EFFICIENCY IN CONSUMPTION
INTENSIVE USE OF PRODUCTS
OPTIMAL LIFE OF PRODUCTS

Source: M. Kostecki (1996)

The concept of *efficiency in consumption* developed by Becker (1965) and Muth (1966) puts the emphasis on household behavior. Consumption is perceived as a process in which a consumer "produces" his satisfaction by combining goods with the available time and know-how. Households, like firms, are constrained in their activities by production technologies. It is suggested that the efficiency of product use can be increased, by education and experience for example. If education may increase an individual's efficiency in production, the same may be said of its impact on efficiency in consumption.

Box 2

Take-back Option
Leaders in client orientation are improving the take-back option offered to their clients. The rationale of that approach, aimed at optimal use of products, is not difficult to grasp. A client purchasing a car is not fully aware of numerous attributes before using it for a week or two. A purchaser of hi-fi. equipment cannot test all the features of the system in the store. Even for products such as textiles, shoes or furniture, clients may realize only after days that the product they bought is not satisfying their needs. An important consumer loss is likely to result from such a situation if no sufficiently generous take-back option is offered to the clients. Recent developments in the consumer protection legislation as well as in the modern distribution favor a generous use of the take-back option.

There is evidence to suggest that an educated consumer will consume, *in ceteris paribus*, as if she were spending more than a less educated consumer. The marketing activities may have a role to play in increasing the efficiency of consumption by informing the consumer, training him in product use, ensuring more optimal adequation between the product attributes and the consumer's needs (e.g. by an improved take-back option) or providing an adequate mix of services around the products.

One of the factors which strengthens a supplier's grip on a client is the customer lock-in effect. Numerous technology-intensive consumer durables are difficult to use, so once a consumer has learnt how to operate a PC, say, he is loth to switch. This favors durable use of products and makes it harder for rivals to compete.

Intensive use of products signifies that the occasions of product use are multiplied. For example, an intensive use of vacation apartments may be encouraged by a periodic rent or a time-sharing arrangement.

The use of consumer durables might also be intensified through improved regulations favoring better access to product use or marketing arrangements encouraging intensive use. An intensive use of a car and its maintenance services might be stimulated by leasing or a legislation stipulating that a car transporting at least two passengers to work benefits from lower fiscal charges than automobiles transporting a single passenger.

Box 3

Intensive Use of Personal and Non-personal Products

A distinction may be made between personal and non-personal products. A tooth brush is a personal product. A given product is personal if the exclusivity of its use is an important determinant of consumer satisfaction.

(1) $Ut = Up - Uc$

where

Ut represents the total utility from use of a product,

Up stands for a utility of an exclusive use of a product, and

Uc is a utility of a shared use of a product.

For personal products Uc is assumed to be negative. It signifies that the disutility of shared use exists. If the absolute value of Uc is substantial compared with the price of the product then the shared use is not likely to occur through the market place. (Note that for certain products such as wine, shared use may be perceived as a contribution to the owner's satisfaction and consequently Uc is assumed to be positive). For a great majority of products an average consumer is ready to share his use in exchange for compensation (e.g. fee or rent). Such products may be referred to as non-personal products.

The existence of non-personal products, which are not shared, may result in a social loss. Indeed, under-utilization implies opportunity costs in terms of an alternative investment, e.g., environment-friendly use. There are several ways in which an intensive use of products may be encouraged:

- non-personal products might be designed for multiple consumer use;
- shared use of non-personal products may be promoted through community work, public policy or regulations making collective use of such facilities as laundry rooms, heating systems, parking spaces, sailing-boats or cars easier;
- communication, promotion and distribution strategies could be designed to favor intensive consumption.

One of the central propositions of this study is that growing concern of optimal use is likely to offer increasingly attractive opportunities for businesses.

2. LIFE OF A PRODUCT

The life span of a product (LP) or durability is a central notion of this study. A schematic presentation of essential stages and options in product life is presented in Figure 1.1.

The LP concept may be visualized in three manners: linear, circular or systemic. Traditionally, marketing has been seen as having a linear construct. Marketing was looked upon as a link in the chain between production and consumption. The main feedback between use and production or R&D was that of information. Product durability was further restrained due to the sales-orientation of marketing activities as well as the weakness of the remarketing system (chapter 3).

The traditional approach is based on a linear reasoning of the following type: production-consumption-waste which is predominant in a mass consumption society (Stahel, ch. 2). In that perspective, R&D activities elaborate products without attaching importance to the real constraints of product use. Products are designed and standardized. Technology is introduced without much concern for the utilization. The client is situated at the end of the chain, rather than at the beginning, and little concern is given to client real preferences other than those which are decisive factors at the moment of the purchase (Kostecki, ch. 3).

Table 1.3

ESTIMATES OF AVERAGE LIFE-TIMES OF CONSUMER DURABLES (Developed Economies, 1990s and 1980s)
BICYCLES 4 – 8 YEARS
CARS 8 – 9 YEARS*
COATS & JACKETS (WINTER) 2 – 5 YEARS**
COOKERS 10 – 15 YEARS***
MICROWAVES OVEN 8 – 10 YEARS
PERSONAL COMPUTER 3 – 5
REFRIGERATORS 8 – 12***
SHOES (WINTER) 2 – 3
TELEPHONES 4 – 6
TV SETS 8 – 10
WASHING MACHINES 7 – 10 ***

Source: Cooper (1994 and 1995), Kisiel Kostecki (ch. 10), Poll (1993) quoted according to Cooper and own estimates.

Notes: * The average life span of a Volvo car in Sweden was above 20 years in 1996.
        ** Substantial differences for men and women. The latter favor lesser durability.
        *** Estimates for Switzerland only.

Figure 1.1   Stages in the Useful Life of a Product

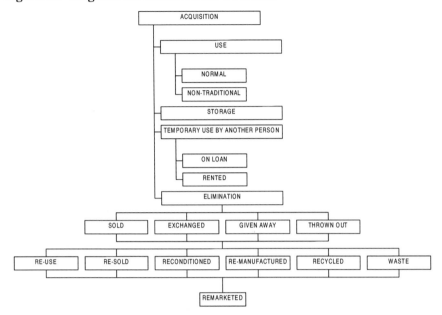

A circular vision was a response to public pressure, regulation and new environmental concerns of the seventies and eighties. It put an emphasis on reuse and recycling and suggests that a movement similar to: production-consumption-recycling-production should be circular as discussed in Chapter 2 below (see Figure 2.2).

Börlin and Stahel (1987) suggest four loops in which the circular life of a product may take place. In the case of a small loop like an immediate product reuse by a new owner (user), the marketing activity will consist of retake and re-marketing of the used product. In loop 2, repair or certain reconditioning will be required (cleaning, labeling, packaging, etc.). The importance of marketing activities as a unifying component of the model are even further expanded in the case where re-manufacturing is needed.

According to Börlin and Stahel efficiency gains may frequently be obtained by moving away from recycling, to smaller loops of direct reuse, reuse after repair or reuse after re-manufacturing. Three basic strategies are suggested to increase the durable use of products to protect the environment through lesser consumption of energy and material as well as waste avoidance:

I.   Product is designed, conceived and produced to last.
II. Product is made to last longer.
    A.   Reuse after control and cleaning (e.g. reutilization of bottles),
    B.   Repair of standard failures (e.g. repair of household equipment),
    C.   Reconditioning to the original state (e.g. tires),
    D.   Up-dating the product's technology (e.g. thermal isolation of old buildings).

III. Reuse of components (e.g. spare parts from the used cars) or reuse of computer microchips in children's toys.

A complementary vision to that of Börlin and Stahel is the Optimal Use System (OUS). In the OUS model, product life is looked upon as a process taking place within a system composed of producers, intermediaries and consumers operating in partnership and aiming at the optimization of both production and use.

Figure 1.2 The Optimal Use System (OUS)

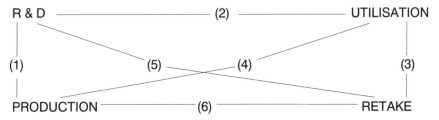

Notes:
(1) Research and development (R&D) and production are fully integrated.
(2) Use-tested design and (3) Use-optimising design (intensive use, efficient use, durable use).
(4) Client-oriented production.
(5) Product is designed taking into consideration the needs of the retake and after-use activities.
(6) Production and after-use activities are integrated.

The producers and intermediaries assume a central role as managers of the optimal use system. The OUS is inspired by a marketing vision which integrates production, use and product handling after use into a single managerial model. The strength of the strategy of optimal use is that it may be a profitable business option, and as such, it is implemented by companies that spot that area as an attractive business opportunity.

The OUS approach relies on the observation that clients buy physical objects for their benefit or service built into those products and that the optimization of use from the consumer perspective provides a window of opportunity for doing business in an economy that is increasingly client-oriented. Consequently, the producers and the intermediaries should structure their activities around client needs and the utilization of the products by the client. A consumer vision of product use should thus provide a starting point for the development of the OUS approach to the life of the product. A schematic presentation of the OUS model optimizing both production and use is included in Figure 1.2.

The OUS approach has the following major characteristics:
(a) Product design, production, marketing, product-handling after use, reuse and re-marketing are integrated into a single model.
(b) The management of the process is based on a partnership involving produc-ers, intermediaries and other providers of "durability" services (e.g. mainte-

nance and repair services) as well as the users. The management of the durability system implies a shared responsibility between the actors involved.

(c) Relationship marketing is one of the basic components of the system since it
constitutes a link between partners of the OUS.

(d) Credibility of the OUS depends critically on the guarantee that the user's
interests are fully taken into account at all the stages of the product's life.
Several types of such guaranties are listed in Table 1.4.

Table 1.4

INTEGRATING USERS' INTERESTS INTO PRODUCT LIFE
PRODUCT CONCEPT IS USE TESTED CONSTANT FEEDBACK BETWEEN R&D AND USE EXTENDED PRODUCT RESPONSIBILITY USERS ARE INVOLVED IN THE R&D AND PRODUCTION DECISIONS

The concepts of the Extended Product Responsibility (EPR) and Product
Stewardship (as briefly presented in Box 4 and discussed in Chapter 4) provide
interesting cases of companies currently moving closer to the OUS concept.

Box 4

Product Stewardship
Digital defines product stewardship as working to minimize product impact on environment, health and safety throughout the entire life-cycle, while maintaining product price/cost, performance and quality standards (Merlot, ch. 9). Rank Xerox considered product stewardship as a major change in its corporate philosophy and a driving force of its environmental performance (Maslennikova, ch. 8). Product stewardship maintains a focus on every stage of a product's life cycle: development and design, procurement of parts and raw materials, manufacturing operations, delivery, customer use/service, recovery from customers at the end of life, remanufacturing, reprocessing of parts and recycling of materials. Once companies became aware of the opportunities in Product Stewardship, they applied that concept not only to the product *per se*, but to the entire business of their firms.

3. SHORT LIFE OF PRODUCTS

The average age of consumer durables in the high income countries has declined
over recent decades. What are the moving forces of that trend? The main reasons
are listed in Table 1.5 below.

Table 1.5

REASONS FOR SHORTER LIFE OF PRODUCTS
• Strategies expanding market size through lesser durability continue to be widely followed.   • Managerial decision-making is biased towards single use.   • Consumers have a preference for novelty.   • Consumers are manipulated to consume faster.   • Higher per capita income reduces consumer's concern with optimal use of products.   • Product/service price ratio has changed to the disadvantage of the repair service.   • Technological progress renders products obsolete.   • It is difficult to communicate the benefits of durability to the consumer.   • Used products have an image problem.   • The systems of retake, remarketing and remanufacturing tend to be archaic and ineffective.

Proposition 1: The circle of ever-increasing production favors lesser durability.

The priority of commercial objectives to sell more over optimal use of products finds its roots in the early XVIII century, when in England buying and selling began to be considered vital for life-giving commerce (Porter, 1993). William Harey's discovery of the circulation of the blood might have inspired the mercantilist credo that opulence grew out of the velocity of commercial transactions and might have fueled the dialectics of wealth and waste.

The vision of "non-durable durables" fits well into the *modus operandi* of the contemporary industrial economy in which a vicious circle of ever-increasing production and consumption continues to operate. At the macro level, economic prosperity is measured by GNP which grows when "non-durable durables" are rapidly replaced by new material goods. At the corporate level, growth continues to provide one of the major criteria of managerial success.

In a context where too many products are chasing too few clients most companies try to expand their size of the market by producing goods that are of lesser than optimal durability. Products are conceived, it is claimed, to be rapidly replaced by new products. Marketing strategies are employed to limit the product life by rendering their symbolic components obsolete (e.g. by accelerating the change of fashion), or by consciously promoting technological obsolescence (see also ch. 3). This perception is confirmed by the results of an empirical investigation of young consumers in the French-speaking part of Switzerland. In this study, 95 % of the consumers interviewed suggested that the durability of clothing has declined over the last fifty years. They considered that the main reason for that trend should be found in the changing fashion, and the impact of publicity, as well as in the producers' strategies which consciously limit product durability (Grandi et al., 1996).

Box 5

The Product Life Cycle
Life of a product is frequently confused with the concept of the product life cycle (PLC). The PLC looks at the life of a product from the perspective of the firm's product portfolio and it centers on opportunities and problems with respect to marketing strategy and profitability of particular product lines of the firm. Product life cycles vary considerably in their shape but typically comprise four basic stages: introduction, growth, maturity, and decline (Goldman, Muller, 1982). When a new product is successful, competitors are quick to copy it and the new product's life is considerably shortened (Kotler, 1991). The durability of product use is of some concern in that context because long product use implies more rapidly saturated markets. It means that fewer old goods are replaced by new ones and that the producers have to move to new geographic or product markets to generate sales opportunities.

Proposition 2: Managerial decision-making is biased in favor of single product use.

Financial models of product costing in many contemporary firms are biased towards limited product use rather than optimal product utilization (WBCSD,1995). Durable design usually leads to higher manufacturing costs and few companies know how to turn those costs into a profitable investment. Consequently, very few companies have traditionally cared about retake, re-manufacturing and re-marketing which contribute to the product's durable use. The concepts of Extended product responsibility (EPR) and the use of a mix of unit manufacturing cost models (that incorporate use and reuse) provide new windows of opportunity for innovative business firms (Charter, ch. 5 and Maslennikova, ch.8).

Proposition 3: Consumers have preference for novelty.

Products are composed of three essential elements: material products, services and symbols. Any satisfactory explanation for the phenomenon of a shortened life of products should include some reference to its symbolic content and to changes in the conduct of consumers (Campbell, 1993). The disease of consumption that is wasteful is the disease of excess. Thomas Beddoes a romantic English writer (see: motto), suggested that the evil of consumerism is a sort of fetishism of culture in which the body is forgotten in the name of fashionable goals (1802). That idea was taken over by Baudrillard who interpreted consumption as an activity in the world of symbols. For numerous analysts, consumers of the mass consumption society have the license to acquire more. For others, the most crucial is the development of new values which help people to transcend that very license to acquire (McCracken, 1988). Pascal observed that a man is strongly influenced by the *charmes de la nouveauté* and the *"cours témérairement après les nouvelles*" (Pensées). This feature of human nature is effectively used in promotion campaigns to increase the velocity of commercial transactions.

Box 6

Fashion and Product Durability
Marketing literature makes a distinction between fad, fashion and style. A style is a distinctive form of human expression of a basic and lasting nature. Distinctive styles may be, for example, identified in art (e.g. art deco), clothing and architecture (e.g. Palladio) or furniture (e.g. Regency style). Most styles tend to last generations but exhibit cycles of growing and declining interest over time.   Fashion may be defined as a style that is currently popular. Its development usually proceeds in stages such as distinctiveness, emulation, mass fashion and decline (Wasson, 1968). The stage in which certain consumers (innovators) take an interest in a novelty to distinguish themselves from others is referred to as the distinctiveness stage. Numerous other consumers (early adopters) follow in the emulation stage. The growing popularity of a particular mode of expression results in the mass-fashion stage. Finally, something else begins to attract the attention of the consumers and the decline stage of the fashion is reached. The length of a particular fashion cycle depends on the fashion's ability to meet genuine consumer needs, to remain consistent with other trends in social life and societal values, as well as with the technological changes taking place (Sproles, 1981). There are several other theories of fashion cycles. A number of them suggest that fashions develop regardless of economic, technological and functional changes in the society (e.g. Robinson, 1975).   Finally, fads are fashions that arrive quickly, become popular and decline very fast. Fads typically don't satisfy a strong need nor do they satisfy it well (Kotler, 1991). Cyclical changes in style such as fads or less rapidly changing fashions reduce the life of products with important symbolic attributes which are modified or eliminated to adjust to the new. The duration of fashions and fads that is shorter than the technical and economic life of a product may result in sub-optimal product utilization if no appropriate systems of re-marketing and reuse are put in place. Empirical results show that the above trend in the area of clothing is particularly important for products such as pullovers, shirts and T-shirts (Grandi et al., 1996).

Proposition 4: Consumers are manipulated to consume faster.

Publicity and promotion reinforce consumer preference for novelty, rendering numerous useable products obsolete well before their technical or functional capacities are fully used. Beginning at least as early as Vance Packard's "The Hidden Persuaders" (1955), a steady stream of publications have pointed out over-consumption and the anti-durability bias of a mass consumption society. It was claimed that consumers were brainwashed to consume more and more of not necessarily what they really needed but what the producers wanted them to. Publicity and promotion were utilized to further reinforce the consumer's natural fascination with novelty (symbol manipulation).

The advantages of product durability are also much harder to "sell" to the consumer than the benefits of product novelty. The messages of "new" constitute a more attractive selling proposition than the benefits of optimal use of products. Two main reasons explain this situation:

First, "new" is appealing in a society where terms such as "change", "youth" or "dynamic" are perceived more positively than in previous generations. The return on the investment in the symbolic value of "new" is higher than that in "durable". That observation combined with the proposition 3 explains why the tendency towards "new" is self-reinforcing.

Second, the consumer's benefits of durable use are complex and more apparent *ex post* than *ex ante*. They may result from lower costs, absence of frustration that could result from the inability to use a new product, or personal attachment to a product that has been around for some time. Product durability may also be linked to attributes such as "eternity", "tradition", "memory", "protection of the environment", "rational buying behavior", "restrain in consumption" "prudent spending," "solid", "personalized", etc. Such communication strategies may be convincing in the case of some products (e.g. luxury watches, furniture or art collections) but not necessarily for other durables that are rendered banal by mass production. More consumer research is needed to clarify for which products durable use is an attractive selling proposition.

Proposition 5: The rise in per capita income reduced consumer's concern with optimal use of products.

Another important eighteen-century novelty was not only the desire to consume but also the ability to do so by larger numbers of the population (de Vries, 1993). Once the basic needs were satisfied, priority was given to the satisfaction of more abstract symbolic attributes (Maslow, 1954). This means more scope for manipulation since commercial communication loses its credibility while it moves away from technical to abstract attributes. Needs that come within ourselves range from basic necessities of survival (primary needs) such as water, salt, food and clothing, to more abstract needs for things such as love, belonging, fulfillment or friendship. Needs are translated into wants relating to a specific means of satisfying a given need, frequently through consumption of commercially acquired goods and services. Abstract needs have no point of satiety. Consumption of affective durables makes us enter the world of symbols which has its own rationality of value creation, consumer choice and a distinctive anatomy of consumer satisfaction (e.g. Baudrillaird, 1968; Richard, 1980; Langer, 1957; Levy, 1959).

Finally the rise in income of consumers has increased the value of their time. Since maintenance services require a lot of consumer time, they reduce the consumers willingness to preoccupy themselves with maintenance of used products.

Proposition 6: Product/service price ratio has changed to the disadvantage of the repair service and has reduced the life of products.

The useful life of consumer durables depends on the price of the maintenance services required to ensure the use of products. The higher, *in ceteris paribus*, the price of the maintenance service, the stronger the tendency to substitute a product requiring repair with a new product (Adler and Hlavacek, 1976). For decades the productivity of maintenance services has been lagging behind the productivity in manufacturing. This is due to a lesser scope for services industrialization and a higher labor-intensity of services. Moreover, many services around products have remained "archaic" because they have been relatively little affected by techno-logical change and protected against competition (Kostecki, 1994). Over the last two decades, the impact of technological change on services has became strong and even determinant, opening new avenues for durability strategies. One of the striking cases for example, is the possibility of providing certain repair services of computer equipment at a distance "on line". An OUS system might offer a realistic option to change the product/service price ratio to a service's advantage.

Proposition 7: Technological progress contributes to render products obsolete.

New technologies render numerous products obsolete both in technical and economic terms. There is strong empirical evidence that over the last half a century the average life of consumer durables has declined largely in response to changes in technology. The percentage of sales of products introduced more than 10 years ago was 27 percent in the mid eighties whereas it was in the range of 15 per cent in the mid-nineties. About 50 years ago the length of a life cycle was in the range of 24 years for pharmaceutical drugs, 20 years for food, 16 years for tools, 14 years for games and about 12 years for cosmetics. The corresponding figures for the early nineties are: 8 years for pharmaceutical drugs, 5 years for food, 4 years for tools 3 years for games and about 3 years for cosmetics (McKin-sey,1995, Siemens,1994). Numerous authors argue that many consumer durables are designed to have uneconomically short life spans, with the intention of forc-ing clients to repurchase more frequently (Coase, 1972, Bulow, 1986, Scitovsky, 1994). This phenomenon is referred to as "planned obsolescence'. Product life cycles continue to shrink in numerous sectors like clothing, furniture, the auto-motive industry or computers. Several new models of vehicles roll out the door every year. Speed in creating new product design is of essence. Coase (1972) and Bulow (1986) argue that such a limited life span of numerous consumer durables is the cost imposed by the monopolistic producers to overcome the time consis-tency problem. Others suggest that planned obsolescence is necessary to achieve technological progress. If products are too durable, 'potential innovators may lack the incentives to invest in the development of a new technology and the economy may stagnate as a result' (Fisherman, Gandal, Oz, 1993).

Optimal life of products with all its implications for waste prevention, envi-ronment and consumption patterns is of little concern in such an environment.

Basically, new technologies are desirable if they are superior. However, that is not always the case. A non-negligible aspect of technology's impact on useful life of products is related to the management power structure and the place of technology experts in it. In companies dependent on technology and innovation the engineers maintain dominant influence in decision-making. There is a fascination with technological change. The change is implemented at all costs as a matter of "innovative strategy", the company's image or technological leadership, etc.. The question is rarely asked as to whether the consumers have equal preferences for the new technology and whether the technological change truly adds to the consumer's value chain. In addition, little regard is paid to the issue of technological compatibility (proposition 3).

Box 7

Product Design and Efficiency in Consumption
Numerous firms wind up selling complex products overloaded with technology that consumers can't figure out. Indeed, consumers often complain about the difficulties of using, computers, VCRs, hi-fi equipment, or even once familiar message machines, copiers or alarm clocks. Modern technology has turned the economics of design on its head. With the extensive use of the microchip, the cost of adding features no longer limits the number of capabilities that a designer can put into a product. The chip that was designed to perform a single basic function can frequently be made to do two, four or even 80 operations at a minimal marginal cost. So, those in charge of R&D pile on the additional features "to make the product appealing" but without asking whether the customers are willing or able to use them. For example, Ricoh Co., one of the leading manufacturers of office equipment in Japan found in the 1991 survey of its fax customers that nearly 95% never used three key functions of their fax machines because they either didn't know these features existed, didn't understand them, or didn't know how to operate the machine (*Business Week*, 29.4.91). Today's consumers are rebelling against the devil of design. If attention is paid to the human interface easy-to-use consumer durables should be supplied in greater numbers.

Proposition 8: Most used products have an image problem.

The image of a "used product" is a disadvantage in marketing. Second-hand goods are perceived as inferior, non-hygienic, risky or less prestigious. Used products rarely benefit from the same quality of packaging and presentation as similar new goods. Companies favoring re-marketing have to develop innovative techniques to deal with the image problem. For certain goods re-manufacturing, guarantee and professional presentation may turn "used" into an advantage. The salesman may for example insist on the product's uniqueness, antiquity, testimony of another epoch, etc. In still other cases, re-used products or components may be presented as essentially equivalent to new equipment. For example, Rank Xerox insists that its remanufactured photocopy machines are not second-hand but goods under full guarantee and comparable in value to new equipment (Maslennikova, chapter 8).

Proposition 9: The systems of retake, re-marketing and re-manufacturing tend to be archaic and ineffective.

To be effective, the systems of retake, re-use and re-marketing should be managed as a client-oriented service operation. Such is rarely the case. A large portion of product retake is based on benevolence and on disciplining the citizen. Motivation schemes are too timidly used to be fully effective. Distribution chains frequently resist retake because they are not properly encouraged into a real and beneficial partnership with the producers and product users. New solutions are needed to introduce modern marketing approaches into that field of activity and to integrate them into the Optimal Use System (OUS).

The above overview allows an identification of a number of forces which are exogenous from a firm's perspective (propositions 3, 5 and 6) and those that are clearly indigenous (e.g. propositions 1, 2, 4 or 9). The distinction is important because business-induced causes of sub-optimal use of products may be removed by modifying the marketing strategies of the firms. The corporate willingness to adopt such new strategies depends on the profitability of the "durable use" options.

4. Consumer Choice and Product Durability

Durable use of products is not a religion. Product durability is not an objective in itself. Is there any reason to suggest that consumer durables should have longer lives? Is our spending on increased product durability justified? Let us briefly consider the major features of consumer choice related to product durability before discussing the benefits of durable use of products.

An overview of consumer behavior with respect to product life and durability is important to marketers because the whole of marketing rests on assumptions about how customers make choices. Therefore, consumer attitude towards product durability, perception of the most important attributes of durable products and willingness to pay for longer product utilization are crucial to businesses envisaging durability-based marketing strategies.

What is the useful (optimal) life of a product? It is variously defined as depending on whether the decision-horizon is that of a producer, consumer or public authority concerned with social costs such as the environmental costs, safety hazards, etc. As the current balance of power in the marketing systems of the advanced countries is changing in favor of the consumer, his interests have to be increasingly taken into account by the producers and the public authorities. Product durability is one of the aspects of that issue.

Consumer choice is not a single act. It is a series of activities that constitute the buying process. The marketing approach which is to serve product durability

should take into account the consumer's choice. The relationship between product durability and consumer choice raises three important questions:
(a) How do consumers use products?
(b) How do consumers view durability?
(c) What "durability" attributes are taken into account (a) in the buying process and (b) in the post-use evaluation (satisfaction) and what is their importance?

Table 1.6

DIMENSIONS OF PRODUCT DURABILITY	
Durability	Determinant
Functional	Product's effectiveness in satisfying consumer's functional needs compared with that of the other (new) available products.
Economic	Product's performance/cost ratio compared with that of the other (new) available products.
Symbolic	Products ability to satisfy abstract needs such as desire for novelty, style, prestige and other aspects of the consumer's image.

Source: M. Kostecki (1996)

The life of a product from a consumer's perspective has several dimensions that can be organized under three principal headings: functional, economic and symbolic aspects of product durability (Table 1.6), e.g., attitude towards durable use of products (is it desirable?), the perception of product durability (criteria on which product durability is evaluated), post-purchase issues of optimal use (such as intensive use, skillful use and services around products), as well as the issue of product re-take, re-manufacturing, re-marketing and re-use.

What is the relationship between the three dimensions of product durability? A certain minimum degree of functionality is a necessary condition of durability in use for most products. However, the condition is not sufficient because economics of use is a superior requirement. It calls for a "useful durability" i.e. one that results in services which make economic sense. Even products that are technically fit and functional may be eliminated on economic grounds.

The relationship between the symbolic dimension on the one hand and the functional or economic dimensions on the other is much less determined. For example, it is not rare that insufficient functionality is accepted for the symbolic reasons (e.g. the use of a collection car).

Box 8

Economic Aspects of Product Replacement
A rational consumer will opt for a new product if the continous utilization of the old product costs more than a replacement with a new product. The following equation determines the condition of consumer choice:

(2) $$\sum_{i=1}^{n} C_i > C_p + C_r \qquad i = (1,....,n) \text{ where,}$$

C_i stands for the differential in the cost of utilization between the used and the newly available product for an activity *i* over a chosen time horizon. (That cost differential is determined by the cost differential in the maintenance services, in the cost of energy, in the cost of labour, etc.);

C_p is the purchasing price of the newly available product adjusted over a chosen time horizon (amortization).

C_r is the cost of retake of the used product.

The above formula suggests that a useful durability may be increased by charging a full price for the retake of used products (C_r) or reducing the costs of the maintenance services (C_i) as compared to the costs of production. Maintenance services tend to be overvalued because of the protective social legislation of labor (maintenance is labor-intensive) whereas, the price of energy used in production tends to be undervalued since it is frequently subsidized or does not take into account the environmental impact of the energy used. Moreover, numerous producers follow the so called "stuck-with-the-product" strategy: the product is initially offered at a reasonable price and prices of the spare parts and services are excessively high. Removal of such systemic distortions is thus likely to result in a more optimal use of products.

Table 1.7

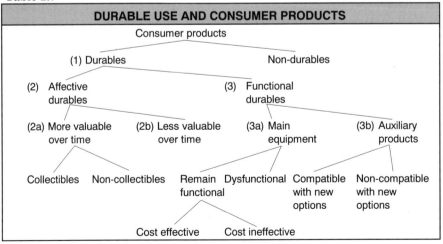

DURABLE USE AND CONSUMER PRODUCTS

A related issue to that of a product's symbolic content is the user's attachment to the product. Certain products should be seen as closely tied to the context of life and the network of social relationships and not viewed uniquely from the standpoint of traits given to them in their industrial production or marketing. Consumers become attached to certain objects because they remind them of people, events or simply because they have been a part of their personal surroundings for a long period of time (symbolic attachment). Individuals also get attached to certain goods because they are familiar with the product's use and are not willing to change their habits (functional attachment).

Box 9

Cars and the Consumer's Nostalgia
Anecdotal evidence may be quoted to illustrate the types of and motivation of consumer's symbolic attachment to numerous products. For example, the German car producer Mercedes Benz re-manufactures certain of its older models from the seventies and eighties offering them under guarantee at a premium price. For example, a remanufactured Mercedes car 230E dating from 1982 was offered for sale in 1994 for DM 24.000, i.e. at about 60 per cent of the (original) nominal selling price. Among the clients the remanufactured vehicles prominently figure numerous professionals such as medical doctors, lawyers, dentists or engineers who remember the Mercedes models from their university days but at that time were not able to afford them (see chapter 11).

Depending on the buying motives and the related characteristics of decision-making, the marketing strategies favoring product durability differ considerably in nature and scope.

Table 1.8

CONSUMER CHOICE AND DURABILITY ATTRIBUTES OF PRODUCTS		
Motives of buying	*Characteristics of decision-making*	*Major concerns*
Utilitarian	Predominance of rational over affective modes of decision-making.	• Cost/benefit of durable use. • Tangible features of durability.
Cognitive	Emphasis on problem-solving, and risk-avoidance.	• Durability as a factor of problem-removal and/or problem- avoidance.
Affective	Product appraisal aimed at satisfying emotional needs for enhancement of social approval or sensory gratification.	• Subjective meanings of durability attributes and intangible features of products. • Image and perceived value.

For example, utilitarian buying will require a product design that emphasizes the tangible qualities of durability such as materials perceived as reliable or of solid construction. Cognitive buying motives require that the clients be well-informed about the virtues of the product to solve their problems. Techniques such as consultative selling, guarantee of performance or training are dominant factors of marketing success. Finally, affective buying signifies that the user's emphasis is to be put on the perceived symbolic value and on the intangible features of durability such as design, style, etc. The leading marketing challenges of durability are discussed in greater detail below.

5. WHAT MARKETING STRATEGIES FOR OPTIMAL PRODUCT USE?

The traditional patterns of thinking about product use and supplier/client relations are breaking down. A new state of mind naturally leads to such concepts as: product stewardship, extended product responsibility, optimal use of products and client-orientation. In order to succeed, businesses have to offer solutions based on the performance of integrated systems rather than individual goods and services. They have to assume more responsibility in the area of product use, retake, re-marketing and re-use.

Any improvements in the field of product durability require a corporate response. Several reasons motivate businesses to give more attention to the issue of the optimal use of products:

Saturation of material product markets. Growth of businesses may take place by increased sales in the traditional market, by developing new markets or by exploiting new product development possibilities. For many material products, the markets of the high income countries are highly saturated. Numerous businesses have to look for either new markets or develop innovative product offers. Offering durability services and assuming a greater responsibility for product use is a particular type of the latter strategy.

A sales response function may be defined as:

$$dV/dt = r\,P(S-V_p)/S + (1+u)\,dV_s/dt$$

where:

$V = V_p + V_s$ stands for sales of material products + sales of services (such as durability services),

r and u are constants of sales responses for material products,

S stands for saturation level for sales of material products,

P is promotion and publicity budget for material products.

It is the offer of improved services around products (second component of the equation) that increasingly constitutes the driving force in the growth of sales.

In modern economies a growing portion of resources is related to the use of services in product utilization and other functions rather than in the purchase of the products. Those services are strategic in the sense that without them hardware ceases to have further value (Giarini, 1996). Services have become an increasingly important source of profits for companies that were traditionally manufacturing firms. Services such as durability services have a double function:

(a) they contribute to the company's sales growth directly (because services are sold);

(b) the increase in the offer of services around products has a promotional impact on the sales of material products.

It is revealing to note that Rank Xerox operations involving retake and re-manufacturing were more profitable in 1995 than the traditional area of manu-facturing of new photocopy machines (Maslennikova, ch. 8).

Service Technology. Technological leaders may have increased return (cost advantage) in certain types of services and turned it into strategic advantage over other competitors. This would result in new entries into certain service industries of companies that are technological leaders in the strategic areas of service technology.

Over the years the sequence of change has run from technological change to product and process innovation in service activities. More recently technological change in services has become more endogenous with service providers increas-ingly assuming the role of innovators. Technologies such as electronics and telecommunication are currently characterized by diminishing returns in many industrial sectors, whereas they are in a phase of increasing returns in numerous service activities such as services around products.

Box 10

Maintenance Self-service
In the early nineties several leading manufacturers of photocopy machines devel-oped a new overall design strategy to render their maintenance services simpler and easier for the user to execute by himself. Anthropologists, sociologists, cogni-tive scientists and repair personnel who actually deal with the users worked to-gether to devise clear graphic displays for the complex copier. The objective was to show the user how to operate the basic functions and to take the user through more complex operations only when requested. Such programs permitted the introduction of touch-screen menus that provided options for easy instructions. It is important for the optimal use of products that if trouble occurs the users be able to understand what went wrong and correct it. It is now widely accepted in the photo-copy equipment sector that a machine must provide the user with tools to manage trouble (see chapter 8).

Protection of the environment. The environment has become an important public concern exceeding the stage of a fashionable trend. Though the fashion for "green" may be gone, corporate strategies have to be increasingly "environment-friendly" because of the necessity of life and legal requirements. Companies must also offer green products because such products are demanded by their clientele. Innovative companies aim at establishing themselves as leaders in the field of environment-friendly behavior. Optimal use of products is an important aspect of such strategies.

Client orientation. The balance of power in the economic systems of the advanced countries is moving to the advantage of the consumers and competition is more and more centered on the client. First, captive markets are less and less frequent as penury of products offered and monopoly are losing ground. The tendency towards privatization and deregulation contributes to this trend. Secondly, naive markets are increasingly limited due to better consumer information, consumer protection and a growing awareness and dislike of various methods of commercial manipulation. Finally, the markets of numerous consumer durables have become increasingly competitive as products tend to be standardized and commodity-like (e.g. PCs, washing machines, TV sets, etc.).

Producers operating in global markets are numerous, efficient, and subjected to a high degree of competitive pressure. The concept of consumer sovereignty is gaining importance in saturated markets. In such a context client orientation is increasingly accepted as a business strategy and is becoming a condition *sine qua non* of marketing success. It implies that the client, his/her needs and product utilization remain in the center of the producers' concerns. Product durability strategy is thus an important aspect of client orientation, not as an abstract concept but as an operational approach to doing business.

Nature of competition. Concepts such as extended product responsibility or product stewardship are expressions of the new trend. Businesses are forced to cooperate in areas such as sustainable product design, retake (which has to be local even if production is centralized) or re-marketing. Companies that cooperate on some projects are competing in other areas. The ability to create and dissolve partnerships is an essential aspect of strategic flexibility. Credibility with clients and relationship marketing are gaining in importance. Durability may constitute an important aspect of system performance and a determinant selling point.

Investing in Leadership. Optimal use of products is one of the major concerns in the context of client-oriented strategies. There is an important advantage in assuming "durability leadership". The argument is briefly summarized in Figure 1.3.

This shows that a company that becomes a leader in the area of optimal use of products may favor stricter legislation and may encourage pressure groups to favor optimal use in order to sell its know-how in the market (e. g. by providing consultancy to businesses on how to introduce the "optimal use" strategies).

Products and Product Design. Threats properly analyzed and approached constitute opportunities. Let's start with the issue of product design. Traditionally, product design, production and product use were separated. The finished design conceived by the design unit was given to the factory, at which point the designers task was over and both the production people and the users were left alone. The recent idea of concurrent design is that designers should work closely with everyone else who will at some point have a stake in the product concerned. After the manufacturers, the users also have their say throughout the design process. Thus, concurrent design requires managerial input. Manufacturing and maintenance have to be represented during every part of the design process. Customers and even those in charge of re-manufacturing and reuse of products should also be included (see also: Charter, ch. 5).

Computer assisted design (CAD) largely facilitates the task. CAD systems allow the designer to take into account the product durability in a more optimal way than before. The CAD system design remains a consistent whole, by re-membering the history of the design. When the change is made, the program goes back to the point in the part's history where the feature being changed first appeared. It makes the change and runs forward through history modifying everything that has to do with the changed feature.

The CAD system provides the designer with one of the greatest advantages in the world of information that can also benefit the optimal use of products. The designer may ask "What if the technical durability of certain parts or of the whole product were increased?". Alternatives can then be considered without actually trying them out. Obviously, information concerning the use of products is to be fed into the system. A good concurrent design may thus render the concept of an optimal use system both operational and flexible.

Figure 1.3   The Dynamics of Leadership in Optimal use of Products

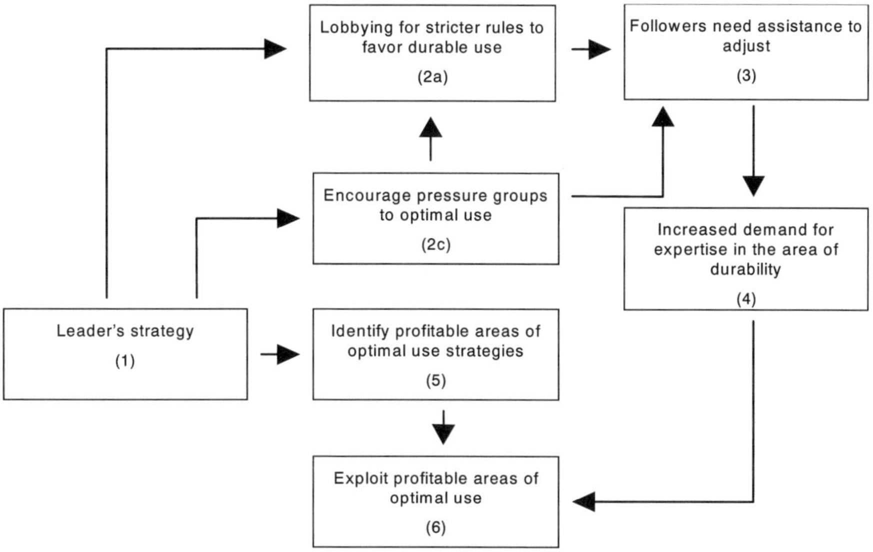

Box 11

Concurrent Design at Boeing
At Boeing, the 777 aircraft design team was composed of experts according to the section of the aircraft they were working on, rather than their functional division in the firm. Customers and service people were also represented. It enabled, for example, British Airways to get four more seats in the 777 Boeing aircraft (i.e., a 1% increase in the plan's capacity) by re-jigging the aft toilets and galleys at no extra cost (The Economist, 5.03.1994).

The sustainability has to be integrated into management and marketing if it is to be practiced. Optimal life of products is an important element of sustainable production and consumption. In order to optimize the use of products it is necessary to link the managerial performance in that area with product design, pricing, distribution, promotion and publicity. It is necessary to find a way of "selling" durable products and making durability a profitable proposition.

One of the lessons drawn from the analysis of cases of retake and re-marketing schemes quoted below is that most of them are archaic or ill-conceived in terms of marketing techniques and approaches. The main managerial concerns in retake and re-marketing are briefly summarized in Table 1.9.

Communication (Publicity and Promotion). Marketing useful durability of products means informing and creating trust. Consumers who consider useful durability an important attribute of certain durables are demanding more information about what goes into products, if the products are designed to last and what services around products are provided to make products durable (chapter 11). How can consumers trust a so-called "durable product" unless they know something about the product composition, performance, guarantees referring to durability and company commitment to manufacturing durable goods.

There are three essential dimensions of the communication challenge related to the useful durability of products: (a) informing the public about the product, its durability and services around the product which ensure durability (durability services); (b) explaining durability in terms of the functional, cost, symbolic and socio-environmental benefits to the consumer; (c) making the durability promise credible (e.g. by providing durability services or granting a guarantee concerning the life span of a product).

Communicating durability successfully not only means creating positive messages and transferring them from a producer to a consumer. Durability communication also signifies that the producer gets involved in the human, social and technical aspects of consumption.

Pricing. Are consumers ready to pay more for durable products? For what category of products is durability a deciding attribute (i.e. one which makes the client chose the product)? How can the price system be designed to provide optimal motivation for partners of the OUS: producers, distributors, users and those in charge of retake, re-marketing and reuse? In that environment are the pricing strategies likely to change in nature? In the traditional context, prices were fixed in relation to production costs and market conditions, whereas in the OUS approach, the pricing of products is similar in nature to the formation of an insurance premium. It takes into account the risks of uncertain events in the future. It is based on a probabilistic evaluation of future costs (or benefits) related to product utilization, retake, re-marketing and resale.

Distribution. The OUS approach opens important new avenues for the distribution systems. The distributors do not only channel the products from the producer to the user but also are in charge of product retake, re-marketing and redistribution. In other terms, the distribution system may assume a strategic role in an OUS arrangement. Important new issues arise in that context for many producers favoring the OUS approach. To what extent should one maintain control over the systems of retake, re-marketing and reuse? What should be the status of the reused products vis-à-vis the status of new goods (e.g. how to deal with the issue of product cannibalism)?

An important aspect of distribution in the OUS approach is that it may provide a counterbalance to the current trend of globalization in production of new material goods. Indeed, many OUS activities are necessarily local in nature. They have to take place close to the client and the local authorities and pressure groups may assume an important role in shaping the OUS schemes.

Table 1.9

MANAGERIAL CONCERNS IN PRODUCT RETAKE AND REMARKETING	
Marketing activity	Managerial Concerns and Issues
Retake	*Criticism*: Too much reliance on benevolence and disciplining of the citizens. Precedence of bureaucracy over client-orientation.
	Issues: What services should be offered and by whom to optimize the retake activities? Who should pay for those services? How does one motivate clients and other participants in the scheme (e.g. retailers, local bottling industry, etc.) to cooperate?
Remarketing	*Criticism*: Most approaches and techniques used in the traditional re-marketing of used products are archaic. Such approaches limit the scope for the economy of scale in re-marketing and result in a non-professional image of re-marketed products.
	Issues: What should the communication strategies be in re-marketing? How does one render the reused products "in"? What guarantees should be offered to increase the perceived value of reused products? What price concessions should be granted to clients? Should we let competitors handle the re-manufacturing and re-marketing of our products?

Source: Based on interviews with 15 managers concerned by retake and re-marketing operations in Switzerland, France, UK and Holland.

7. CONCLUSIONS

The bulk of the existing marketing arrangements for product and packaging retake and re-marketing are archaic in nature. They are for the most part based on benevolence, citizens' discipline and cohesive regulations with little regard being paid to client benefit and dealing with consumer needs for effective services in this area. Many retake and re-use schemes are only vaguely inspired by marketing approaches and techniques.

Sustainable product design favoring optimal durability and product use is gaining in importance because it:
- emphasizes performance and client satisfaction rather than quantitative consumption,
- opens new business opportunities to service clients and to integrate specific offers into more comprehensive systems providing solutions to clients' problems,
- intensifies partnership between producers and their customers based on confidence, interaction and long-term mutual commitment,
- protects the environment through less waste and innovative, more intensive use of products supplemented by durability services.

Leaders in the area of waste avoidance and client-orientation – both large and small firms – have put in place strategies optimizing the useful life of products and product use. A lot may be learned in that area from industrial marketing where the idea of optimal use of products is more widely accepted and techniques such as optimal replacement policy (ORP) were already developed decades ago.

Marketing has a central role to play in the improvements aiming at optimal use of products. The issue of optimal use of consumer durables is likely to remain one of the main challenges of modern marketing systems in the coming decades.

BIBLIOGRAPHY

ADLER, L. and HLAVACEK, J. (1976) "The Relationship between Price and Repair Service for Consumer Durables" *Journal of Marketing*, vol. 40, pp. 80-82.

BECKER, GARY S. (1965) "A Theory of the Allocation of Time", *Economic Journal*, vol. 75, September, pp. 493-517.

BECKER, GARY S. (1971) *Economic Theory*, New York, Alfred A. Knopf, Inc.

BEDDOES, THOMAS LOVELL (1832) *Hygeta*, Bristol, Phillips, vol. 2, p.100.

BÖRLIN, MAX and STAHEL, WALTER (1987) *Stratégie économique de la durabilité*, Zurich, Société de Banque Suisse.

BAUDRILLARD, JEAN (1968) *Le système des objets*, Paris, Gallimard.

CAMPBELL, COLIN (1993) "Understanding Traditional and Modern Patterns of Consumption in Eighteenth-century England: A Character-action Approach" in *Consumption and the World of Goods*, Brewer, John and Peter, Roy (eds.), London and New York, Routledge, pp. 40-57.

COOPER, TIM (1994) "The Durability of Consumer Durables", *Business Strategy and the Environment*, vol. 3, no. 1, pp. 23 – 31.

COOPER, TIM (1994) *Beyond Recycling: The Longer Life Option*, London, New Economics Foundation, 15 p.

COOPER, TIM (1996) *Poor People, Poor Products?* XIVth International Home Economics and Consumer Studies Research Conference, Roehampton Institute, September

DI GENNARO, MONICA and VENTIMIGLIA, PATRIZIA (1996) *La durabilité dans l'emballage*, Mémoire de licence en marketing, Université de Neuchâtel.

FISCHMAN, ARTHUR, GANDAL, NEIL, OZ, SHY (1993) 'Planned Obsolescence as An Engine of Technological Progress' *The Journal of Industrial Economics*, vol. XVI, no. 4.

GIARINI, ORIO (1996) "The Saga of the Service Economy" in *Progres Newsletter*, May 1996, pp. 4-6.

GIARINI, ORIO (1994) "The Service Economy: Challenges and Opportunities for Business Firms" in *Marketing Strategies for Services*, Michel Kostecki (ed.), Oxford, Pergamon Press, pp. 23-40.

GIARINI, ORIO, STAHEL, WALTER (1989) *The Limits to Certainty: Facing Risks in the New Service Economy*, Dordrecht, Kluver Academic Publishers,

GIRARDBILLE, PATRICIA (1995) *La durée de vie des produits: une analyse marketing*, Mémoire de licence en marketing, Université de Neuchâtel.

GIRARDBILLE, PATRICIA and KOSTECKI, MICHEL (1996) "Stratégies marketing et durabilité des produits: Cas et applications", *Cahiers de Recherche en Marketing & Management*, Université de Neuchâtel, CR-MM-96-02, 22p.

GOLDMAN, ARIEH and MULLER, EITAN (1982) *Measuring Shape Patterns of Product Life Cycles: Implications for Marketing Strategy*, Discussion Paper, Jerusalem, Jerusalem School of Business Administration, Hebrew University.

GRANDI, MICHELA and UDRIOT, FLORENCE (1996) *La durabilité des vêtements perçue par les étudiants de Suisse Romande*, Mémoire de licence en marketing, Université de Neuchâtel.

KOSTECKI, MICHEL (1994) "Nouvelles tendances du marketing des services" *Revue Française du Marketing*, no. 149, 1994/4, pp. 25-31.

KOSTECKI, MICHEL (1994 a) Strategies for Global Service Markets, *Marketing Strategies for Services: Globalization, Client-orientation, Deregulation*, M. Kostecki (ed.), Oxford, Pergamon, pp.3-21.

KOSTECKI, MICHEL (1995) "Product Durability: A Roadmap of Challenges" *Cahier de recherche en marketing & management*, Université de Neuchâtel, CR-MM-95-05, 10p.

KOTLER, PHILIP (1991) *Marketing Management*, Engle Cliffs, Prentice- Hall International, Inc.

LANGER, S. (1957) *Philosophy in a New Key*, Cambridge, Harvard University Press.

LEVITT, THEODOR (1981) "Marketing Intangible Products and Product Intangibles" *Harvard Business Review*, vol. 59, May-June 1983, pp. 92-102.

LEVY, S (1959) Symbols for Sale, *Harvard Business Review*, July-August.

MASLOW, A. (1954) *Motivation and Personality*, New York, Harper & Row, pp. 41-2.

MUTH, R. F. (1966) "Household Production and Consumer Demand Functions", *Econometrica*, vol. 34, pp. 699-708.

NIEUWENHUIS, PAUL and WELLS, PETER (eds.) (1994) *Motor Vehicles in the Environment*, Chichester, John Wiley.

PACKARD, VANCE (1955) *The Hidden Persuaders*, New York, Columbia University Press.

POLL, A.J. (1993) *The Recycling and Disposal of Domestic Electrical Appliances*, Warren Spring Laboratory, Stevenage.

PORTER, ROY (1993) "Consumption: Disease of the Consumer Society" in *Consumption and the World of Goods* , Brewer, John and Peter, Roy (eds.), London and New York, Routledge, pp. 58-64.

ROBINSON, DWIGHT E. (1975) "Style Changes: Cyclical, Inexorable and Foreseeable", *Harvard Business Review*, November/ December, pp. 121-131.

SARSON, S. C. (1992) *The Recycling of Electronic Scrap*, Warren Spring Laboratory, Stevenage.

SCITOVSKY, TIBOR (1994) 'Towards a Theory of Second-hand Markets' *Kyklos*, vol. 47, Fasc. 1.

SPROLES, GEORGE B. (1981) "Analyzing Fashion Life Cycles – Principles and Perspectives", *Journal of Marketing*, Fall, 116-124.

DE VRIES, JAN (1993) "Between Purchasing Power and the World of Goods: Understanding the Household Economy in Early Modern Europe" in *Consumption and the World of Goods*, Brewer, John and Peter, Roy (eds.), London and New York, Routledge, pp. 85-132.

WASSON, CHESTER R. (1968) "How Predictable Are Fashion and Other Product Life Cycles?" *Journal of Marketing*, July pp. 36-43.

WBCSD (1995) *Sustainable Production and Consumption: A Business Perspective*, World Business Council for Sustainable Development, Geneva.

CHAPTER 2

PRODUCT DURABILITY AND RE-TAKE AFTER USE

WALTER R. STAHEL

Director, The Product-Life Institute, Geneva

The key to improved product durability lies in the transformation of the actual linear production-focused industrial economy into a utilization-focused service economy operating in loops. Such a transformation process will result in an increased regional competitiveness and a new economic structure relying more extensively on digital and virtual goods rather than the analog (mechanical) products.

This trend towards a more sustainable society and service economy started some time ago, yet most experts are unaware of the potentially fundamental changes that the signs on the horizon indicate. This may be due to an interpretation of the signs in terms of the industrial economy in earlier thinking.

The new service economy needs an appropriate structure, characterized by a regionalization of 'hardware' jobs and skills (mini-mills for material recycling, re-manufacturing workshops for products, decentralized services for maintenance and product-life extension, and do-it-yourself for digital/virtual goods). The latter are supplemented by centralized (or virtual) 'software' jobs and skills (design, research and management centers) which commute by means of electronic highways. Such an economy will consume less resources and have a higher resource productivity. It will be also characterized by smaller units using a possibly more skilled labor input. Transport volumes of material goods will diminish, and be increasingly replaced by transport of immaterial goods.

1. SUSTAINABILITY: WHAT SHOULD CHANGE?

The present industrial economy, which has developed over the last 200 years in today's industrialized countries, is based on the optimization of the production process. It aims to reduce unit costs and thus overcome the scarcity of goods of all kinds, , which was the norm 200 years ago, from food to shelter to durable goods. Emphasis is on efficient process technologies, and a better quality of the

M. Kostecki (ed.) The Durable Use of Consumer Products, 29–39.
© 1998 Kluwer Academic Publishers. Printed in Great Britain.

goods at the moment of sale.

There are indications that the industrial economy is no longer efficiently catering to our needs:

(a) the part of goods that go directly from production to disposal (zero-life products in Figure 2.1) has reached 30% in some sectors;

(b) the number of goods that are disposed of is comparable to the number of goods sold, for many products, indicating a substitution of wealth rather than an increase in wealth;

(c) technological progress is still focused on production, and not on utilization;

(d) for many goods, increases in efficiency through system break-down are comparable to increases in efficiency through product innovation (e.g. safety through traffic jams vs. air bags).

There are also indications that the industrial economy itself is incompatible with the aims of a sustainable society:

• the 'time' factor: sustainability is a *long-term* societal vision, concerned with the stewardship of natural resources (stock equals wealth) in order to safeguard the opportunities and choices of future generations. The industrial economy is a *short-term* optimization of throughput in monetary terms. Changing course towards a more sustainable society means introducing the indeterministic 'time' factor into economic thinking. This in turn implies an indeterministic vision of economics.

• resource productivity: in the linear structure of the industrial economy success, is directly coupled with both matter and energy resource flows. Such an economy might be called a *'river economy'* (Figure 2.1). But a generalization of the present *per capita* resource consumption of industrialized countries is not possible without a collapse of the system. In order to be sustainable, the economy must therefore operate at a much higher level of resource productivity, i.e. be able to produce the same utilization value out of a greatly reduced resource throughput. Such an economy might be called a *'lake economy'* (Figure 2.2). It has been calculated that industrialized countries need to reduce their resource flows by a factor of 10, in order to enable the Less Developed Countries to multiply their *per capita* resource input within a sustainable level of world resource flows (Carnoules declaration of the Factor 10 club). Changing course towards a more sustainable society means to de-couple economic success from resource throughput. One way of doing it is to change to a service economy, in which the measure of results refers mainly to stocks and their utilization, instead of their flows (Giarini and Stahel, 1989 and 1993).

• social and cultural ecology: the industrial economy has been largely *technology*-focused, using *monetarized values* as its main yardstick. A sustainable society is result-focused and based on *social and cultural values (non-monetary assets)*, integrated with economic values. Changing course towards a more sustainable society means to take into account social and cultural factors as peers to economic ones.

A service economy is fundamentally different from the industrial economy in that its main objective is to maintain or increase total wealth and welfare, i.e. the monetary and non-monetary assets of society over long periods of time. Its focal point is the optimization of utilization, i.e. of the performance and the results achieved with goods, rather than the goods themselves.

Figure 2.1 The Linear Structure of the Industrial Economy (or 'River' Economy)

→ zero-life-products →
Resources → base materials → manufacturing→p.o.s. → utilization→waste
junction 0: product-life or waste

Source: Stahel, Walter and Reday, Geneviève (1976/1981) Jobs for Tomorrow, the potential for substituting manpower for energy; report to the Commission of the European Communities, Brussels / Vantage Press, N.Y.

The central notion of economic value in the service economy is the value of utilization over time, in contrast to the value of exchange at the time of sale. (The added value system is only a subsystem of a larger economic concept). Similarly, quality in the service economy is defined as long-term optimization of system functioning, and not as a momentary quality at the time of sale.

Figure 2.2 Closing the Material Loops

The loops of a self-replenishing, more sustainable service economy (or 'lake' economy), and the junctions between these loops and a linear economy

junction 1: product-life extension v. new goods
cost advantage product-life extension

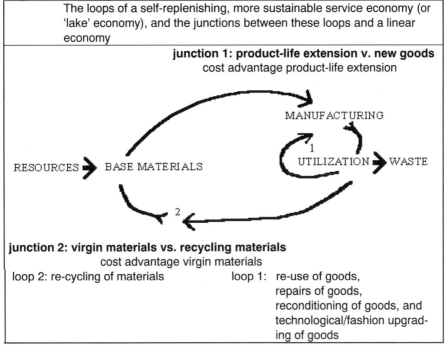

junction 2: virgin materials vs. recycling materials
cost advantage virgin materials

loop 2: re-cycling of materials   loop 1: re-use of goods,
repairs of goods,
reconditioning of goods, and
technological/fashion upgrading of goods

Source: Stahel, Walter and Reday, Geneviève (1976/1981) Jobs for Tomorrow, the potential for substituting manpower for energy; report to the Commission of the European Communities, Brussels / Vantage Press, N.Y.

Figure 2.3 Closing the Liability Loops

The economic optimization of loops only becomes an economic objective if the (invisible) liability loops are closed (take-back of unwanted goods and materials by their manufacturer)
junction 3: asset management vs. waste management
profit maximization in re-use vs. cost minimization in recycling and disposal

The invisible hand of the free market prefers junction 2 to the economically advantageous junction 1, if forced to recycle. It is due to the system's natural preference for throughput optimization and to the lack of national legislation for closed liability loops (product take-back and product stewardship 'from cradle back to cradle' by manufacturers) as well as closed material loops. The latter are 'invisible' and thus easy to forget in a technology-focused economy.

A transition from a resource-flow-based industrial economy to a wealth-management-based service economy will be greatly facilitated if a majority of people and governments can agree on a common vision of sustainability. Such a vision, however, is almost by definition more cultural than technological; furthermore, it needs a clear structure to avoid misinterpretations.

2. THE PILLARS OF A SUSTAINABLE SOCIETY

The concept of 'sustainability' is based on several techno-economic pillars, each of which is essential for the 'survival' of the natural eco-system, of which mankind partakes, on Earth. It is useless to argue on priorities, or speculate on which of these pillars can be lost first; society cannot take the risk of losing a single one of them:

1. *Nature conservation*, or the eco-support system for life on the planet. This pillar contains global aspects (e.g. oceans and atmosphere as global commons, bio-diversity), as well as regional ones (e.g. drinking water, the carrying capacity of nature with regard to populations and their lifestyle).
2. *Health and safety* (non-toxicology, qualitative): a danger mainly related to the health of people and animals, resulting increasingly from man's own activities (e.g. accumulation of toxic substances in the environment such as DDT, mercury or Thalidomide).
3. *Reduced flows of resources*, or higher resource productivity (quantitative, e.g. CO_2): This represents a potentially radical change for the planet (towards a re-acidification and/or climate change), and thus a threat to man's life on Earth. It is also a factor of disequilibrium between economies in the North and the South.

The 'Quest for a Sustainable Society', however, must be much broader and include the longevity and sustainability of our non-techno-economic structures:

4. *Social ecology*, the fabric of societal structures: this pillar includes issues such as democracy, peace, human rights, employment, social integration, security and safety.
5. *Cultural ecology,* which includes education and knowledge, ethics and culture, as well as values of national heritage at the level of the individual, the corporation and the State: 'Show to others that you are able to care, for example by looking after your car or your house (instead of buying a new one)' (IDSA 1995); 'Good engineering and industrial design has always also been ecologically responsible' (Siemens PC 1985); 'Only people, not robots, can permanently improve product quality' (Toyota's labor-intensive assembly lines in the RAV4-factory, 1995); 'Waste is inefficient and therefore un-Japanese' (MITI 1995) (sources of quotes: John P. Kusz, IDSA, 1995; Siemens PC engineers, 1985; Toyota's president on opening the labor-intensive assembly lines in the RAV4-factory, 1995; MITI report, 1995).

Historic examples of sustainability are: (i) the native Americans' rule of 'everything you do should have positive repercussions on the next seven generations', and (ii) the Prussian management rules for sustainable forestry. Both rules are at least 200 years old, and are based on traditional values and a socio-cultural ecology rather than technological ecology.

The precautionary principle, one of the key principles agreed upon in the Rio Declaration (agreed upon during the 1992 UN Conference on Environment and Development), is also primarily based on socio-cultural values – but it has hardly been put into practice so far.

The question therefore arises if modern society, based on legal frameworks and penal systems, can find a recipe for sustainability in areas where precaution is the most efficient (or only) strategy, such as the global commons, without falling victim to 'the prisoners' dilemma' (where each individual fares better than his or her inmates by ruthlessly exploiting his or her personal advantage, but where the prisoners as a whole are better off by cooperating with each other).

The holistic vision of a sustainable society was already at the base of the movement that coined the English term 'sustainability' in the early '70s: the Woodlands Conferences in Houston, Texas, and the related Mitchell Prize Competition (Coomer, 1981). In order to understand the necessity for changing course towards a more sustainable economy, it is vital to keep in mind the wider reference of a sustainable society (including issues such as full and meaningful employment or quality of life).

The first three pillars (see above) form the techno-centric view of a sustainable economy; together with the pillars no. 4 and 5, they form the base for a sustainable society. The inherent problem is that a common international acceptance can probably only be found for pillars 1 to 3. Pillars 4 and 5, the social and cultural ecology, however, are rooted in regional structures, and have to be accepted through tolerance and the principle of regional subsidiary – but they are probably a precondition for the techno-economic sustainability.

3. SUSTAINABLE SOCIETY AS A COMMON GLOBAL VISION

The vision of sustainability should be based on a global consensus, and like the concentric waves in a lake after a stone has been thrown into the water, develop from a few abstract key issues or principles towards a multitude of increasingly concrete and regionally adapted applications:

Vision
Objectives
Industrial policy
Business strategies and management tools
Industrial design for ecological solutions (goods and services).

This process of back-casting from a defined vision has, for instance, been successfully used by the Dutch Sustainable Technology Development programme to identify new domains of future innovation.

The following structure is a more detailed example of these concentric waves, focused on the objective of a higher resource productivity (i.e. pillar 3):

The Common Vision: sustainability.

    Objective: to build and improve all pillars of a sustainable society, including a considerably higher resource productivity.

    Industrial Policy: to promote a self-responsibility of economic actors for example through closed liability and material loops, an extended result-focused product responsibility by economic actors, free-market safety-nets (e.g. mandatory insurance cover), and a legal framework (including taxation) fostering sustainable solutions (goods and services).

    Business Strategies: to develop innovative technical and marketing strategies which identify and optimize sustainable and economically viable solutions "from cradle back to cradle", with the aim to provide customer satisfaction over long periods of time, interpreting quality as a long-term optimization.

    Management Tools: to optimize asset management, resource productivity and risk management, including relevant controlling instruments; and to define benchmarks and methods to measure improvements towards sustainability.

Design for eco-solutions,
goods and services: zero-options (sufficiency), system solutions, and utilization optimization through a longer and more intensive utilization (efficiency), dematerialized solutions (eco-products).

Details of business and design strategies which lead towards more sustainable solutions are given in Figure 2.4.

Reality, in other words, short-term business optimization, has led to the opposite trend of creating concentric waves from the outside inwards: first on the market were 'green' products (each with its own reference frame), followed by services for 'greening businesses' promoted by consulting firms (eco-labels and eco-audits) – even before an agreement on a common vision is in sight.

4. WEALTH WITHOUT RESOURCE CONSUMPTION

The objective of 'wealth without resource consumption' is obviously of little interest to the industrial (river) economy, as it will lead to "economic disaster" (as measured in resource throughput). There is therefore a considerable untapped potential of technical innovation and economic activity ahead for pro-active entrepreneurs that recognize and successfully develop this potential.

The key to 'wealth without resource consumption' is in a service economy: if customers pay an agreed amount per unit of service (and service equals customer satisfaction), service providers have an economic incentive to reduce resource flows, as this will increase their profits doubly: first by reducing procurement costs for materials and energy, and then by reducing waste elimination costs [Giarini, 1980 and 1994]. Examples of this are the Xerox life-cycle design programme for photocopiers (Chapter 8), the re-treading of tyres, the elevator business, Speno's rail-grinding services, Du Pont's voluntary programme to re-take and recycle nylon carpets, ICI's water-lily polyurethane programme, and re-manufacturing activities in general.

The main benefits for pre-active entrepreneurs are a higher long-term competitiveness through reduced costs, higher product quality and customer loyalty, as well as a 'greener' image. The main risk is the increased uncertainty due to the introduction of the 'time' factor into the economic calculation. The latter can, however, be substantially reduced by appropriate design strategies, such as a modular system design for interoperability and compatibility between product families, component standardization for ease of re-use, remanufacture and recycling, and finally loss and abuse prevention built into products (Chapter 5).

Sufficiency is one strategy for higher sustainability and wealth without resource consumption. Think of a hotel: by offering its guests to 'save the environment' by re-using towels for several days, the hotel does indeed reduce the consumption of water, detergents and washing machines. It also reduces its laundry costs and extends the useful life of towels and washing machines, thus increasing its profit margin. Zero-options, or sufficiency, are among the most ecologically efficient solutions – and they also offer the highest savings.

Figure 2.4 Demand and Supply Strategies for a Higher Resource Productivity

Increased resource productivity through:	Type of strategies:	
	closing the material loops technical strategies	**closing the liability loops** commercial / marketing strategies
sufficiency solutions (demand side)	near ZERO-OPTIONS *ploughing by night*	ZERO-OPTIONS *towels in hotels non-insurance rear-end accident*
system solutions reducing *volume and speed* of the resource flow (supply side efficiency)	SYSTEM-SOLUTIONS *Krauss-Maffei PTS plane transport system, skin solutions, accessibility*	SYSTEMIC SOLUTIONS *lighthouses, selling results instead of goods, selling services instead of goods*
more intensive utilization of goods reducing the *volume* of the resource flow: (supply side efficiency)	ECO-PRODUCTS *dematerialized goods, multifunctional goods.*	ECO-MARKETING *shared utilization of goods, selling utilization instead of goods*
longer utilization of goods reducing the *speed* of the resource flow: (supply and demand side efficiency)	RE-MANUFACTURING *long-life goods, service-life extension of goods and of components, new products from waste.*	RE-MARKETING *dis-curement services, away-grading of goods, marketing of fashion up-grades for goods in the market.*

Source: adapted from: Giarini, Orio and Stahel, Walter R. (1989/1993) The Limits to Certainty, Facing Risks in the New Service Economy; Kluwer Academic Publishers, Dordrecht, Boston.

Systems solutions and the shared utilization of goods are also very effective efficiency strategies of higher resource consumption. A number of people sharing in the utilization of a pool of goods can draw the same utilization value through a more intensive use of a substantially reduced number of goods, thus achieving a higher resource productivity per unit of service. Examples of this, aside from public infrastructures such as lighthouses, roads, concert halls and railways, are the Lufthansa car pool for flight crews, the 'Charter Way' concept by Mercedes for trucks, and the textile leasing of materials such as uniforms, towels and hospital linen.

A shared utilization is possible in the (monetarized) economy through rental services and the sale of services instead of goods (laundry and dry cleaning). It is also possible within communities (non-monetary) through lending and sharing. The former takes place within the legal framework of society while the latter's principles of sharing and caring are based on community values (trust and tolerance) which are part of socio-cultural ecology. Some of the issues involved in the sharing of immaterial and material goods are open to misinterpretation because they incorporate values of both society (law) and community (trust). Distrust leads to increased individual consumption, conflict or failure *(3)*.

A shared utilization of *immaterial* goods has two major advantages. Firstly, a great number of people can profit from the goods simultaneously – in contrast to material goods. Secondly, immaterial goods are by definition dematerialized. The technology shift from analog to digital or virtual goods will further enhance shared utilization, even if the main reason for the change to virtual goods is competitiveness, and not ecology.

Product-life extension services of analog (mechanical) goods lead to a regionalization of the economy. On the other hand, digital and virtual goods enable producers to stay global, by providing solutions (such as the technological upgrading of goods) through do-it-yourself activities. This gives producers direct access to the customer; it also eliminates distributors and distribution costs. The coming change to digital television, accompanied by long-life hardware combined with later technological upgrading through software, is an example of such a trend, pushed by the novel German take-back legislation for electronic goods.

Wealth with less resource consumption is further possible by substituting maintenance-free long-life products which deliver high-quality results for disposable products. Modern examples include music CDs (Compact Discs), and supercondensers instead of batteries in electrical goods. CDs are also a point in case for the resulting shift in income from manufacturers to distributors (secondhand sales and rental shops), if the manufacturers themselves do not become service providers (e.g. selling music instead of CDs). The latter option would have demanded a structural change from global manufacturing to local rental services.

A longer utilization of goods through product-life extension services (loop 1 in Figure 2.2), as well as dematerialized product design, also increases resource productivity but needs to be promoted as it goes against the logic of the linear economy. Doubling the useful life of goods reduces by half the amount of resource input and waste output, and in addition reduces the resource consumption in all related services (distribution, advertising, waste transport and disposal) by 50%.

Furthermore, product-life extension services are often a substitution of manpower for energy, and of local workshops for (global) factories, thus enhancing social ecology. Economic success comes through an understanding of the logic inherent in a 'lake economy' based on services. The optimization of utilization demands a proximity to the customer, and thus a regionalization of the economy. As the stock of goods in the marketplace is the new focus of economic optimization (the assets), these goods become the new 'mines' for resources. They cannot economically be centralized as an efficient service economy has to have a decentralized structure (service centers, re-manufacturing workshops and mini-mills).

Service centers ideally are accessible 24 hours a day, such as the emergency department of a major hospital.

5. BENEFITS FOR THE USER CUM CONSUMER

'Service is the ultimate luxury', according to a publicity by the Marriott hotel group. The shift to a service economy (e.g. product rental instead of purchase) encounters very few problems of acceptance on the demand side. The consumer turned user gains a lot of flexibility in the utilization of goods (something owner-ship can never give him), as well as guaranteed satisfaction at a guaranteed cost per unit of service. Also, there is no loss of status; the marketing of the industrial economy has wrongly created the idea that a status symbol value is linked to ownership – in reality, it has always been linked to leasehold. The driver of a red Ferrari gets the same attention from bystanders if he has bought, rented or stolen the car. Ownership therefore only makes economic sense in cases where durable goods increase in value, normally through an increase in rarity, such as antique furniture, vintage cars and real estate.

Ownership only makes ecological sense for individuals interested in asset management. In many countries, an increasing part of individuals live mentally in a multi-option society. They do not want to commit themselves for medium or long-term, neither to goods nor to people [Gross, 1995]. They want new toys all the time – and can afford them. Only a service economy can fulfill the needs of such consumers without creating an avalanche of waste, by offering them results (use of goods) and services instead of goods as well as flexibility in utilization instead of bondage by property.

Most of these strategies of a higher resource productivity also offer the cus-tomer a reduction in costs. Sufficiency solutions based on a better (scientific) understanding of a problem reduce resource flows and costs: ploughing by night, for instance, reduces weeds and thus herbicide costs by 90%. Remanufactured goods costs on the average 40% less than equivalent new goods of the same quality (Chapter 8). Sharing goods also means sharing costs, but sufficiency and efficiency solutions often demand that the users cum customers develop a new relationship with goods and/or people. Knowledge and community become substitutes for resource consumption.

BIBLIOGRAPHY

Carnoules Declaration of the Factor 10 Club (1994); available from Prof. Dr F. Schmidt-Bleek, Vice-President, Wuppertal Institute, D-42103 Wuppertal.

COOMER, JAMES C. (ed.) (1981) *Quest for a Sustainable Society*, published in cooperation with The Woodlands Conference; Pergamon Press, New York, Oxford etc; ISBN 0-08-027168-5.

DIEREN, WOUTER VAN (1995) *Taking Nature into Account*, Birkhäuser-Verlag, Basel,

ISBN 3-7643-5173-X.

GIARINI, ORIO (1980) *Dialogue on Wealth and Welfare – A Report to the Club of Rome*, Oxford, Pergamon Press, 1980.

GIARINI, ORIO and STAHEL, WALTER R. (1989/1993) *The Limits to Certainty: Facing Risks in the New Service Economy*; Kluwer Academic Publishers, Dordrecht, Boston, London – ISBN 0-7923-2167-7.

GIARINI, ORIO(1994) 'The Service Economy: Challenges and Opportunities for Business Firms', in *Marketing Strategies for Services*, Michel Kostecki (ed.), Oxford Pergamon Press, pp. 23 – 40. – ISBN 0 08 042389 2

GROSS, PETER (1995), *Die Multi-Options-Gesellschaft* (the multi-option society), Suhrkamp Verlag.

GRUHLER, WOLFRAM (1990) *Dienstleistungsbestimmter Strukturwandel in deutschen Industrieunternehmen*; Deutscher Instituts Verlag Köln; ISBN 3-602-24406-7.

JACKSON, TIM (ed.) (1993) *Clean Production Strategies: Developing Preventive Environmental Management in the Industrial Economy* – Stockholm Environment Institute; Lewis Publishers, Boca Raton, Ann Arbor, London, ISBN 0-87371-884-4.

JACKSON, TIM(1996) *Material Concerns, Pollution, Profit and Quality of Life*; Routledge, London. ISBN 0-415-13249-5.

JETRO (1992) *Ecofactory – Concept and R&D Themes – New Technology Japan*; Japan External Trade Organization, Special Issue JETRO FY 1992.

SCHMIDT-BLEEK, FRIEDRICH (1994/96) *The Fossil Makers – Factor 10 and More* (Wieviel Umwelt braucht der Mensch? MIPS – Das Mass für ökologisches Wirtschaften); Birkhäuser Verlags AG, Berlin, Basel; ISBN 3-7643-2959-9.

STAHEL, WALTER R. (1995) 300 examples of higher resource productivity in today's industry and society (Intelligente Produktionsweisen und Nutzungskonzepte) – Handbuch Abfall 1 – Allg. Kreislauf- und Rückstandswirtschaft; Band 1 und 2, Landesanstalt für Umweltschutz Baden-Württemberg (Hrsg.), Karlsruhe.

STAHEL, WALTER R.(1994) The impact of shortening (or lengthening) of life-time of products and production equipment on industrial competitiveness, sustainability and employment; report to the European Commission, DG III, Nov 1, 1994.

STAHEL, WALTER R.(1992) Re-use and Re-cycling, Waste prevention and resource savings in utilization, conference manuscript, Guildford

STAHEL, WALTER R.(1985) Hidden innovation, R&D in a sustainable society, in: Science & Public Policy, Journal of the International Science Policy Foundation, London; Volume 13, Number, 4 August 1986, Special Issue: The Hidden Wealth.

STAHEL, WALTER R.(1984) "The Product-Life Factor"; in: Orr, Susan Grinton (ed.) An Inquiry into the Nature of Sustainable Societies: The Role of the Private Sector; HARC, The Woodlands, TX.

CHAPTER 3

PRODUCT DURABILITY AND MARKETING STRATEGIES

MICHEL KOSTECKI

Director, The Enterprise Institute, University of Neuchâtel

This chapter identifies a road-map of challenges confronting both businesses and government policies in the area of optimal life of consumer durables.

How does the current evolution of markets, marketing practices and consumer preferences in high-income countries affect product durability? What are its implications for corporate strategies and public policies? What options are most promising for reducing environmental waste related to the sub-optimal life of products?

1. BUSINESS STRATEGY AND USEFUL LIFE OF PRODUCTS

Marketing literature (e.g. Kotler, 1991, Vandermerwe,1994) distinguishes several approaches guiding a firm's relationship with its markets: (i) product-centric strategy, (ii) cost-centric strategy, (iii) sales-oriented strategy and (iv) client-oriented strategy.

Product-Centric Strategy

The firm puts most of its energy into making solid, durable hardware. It is assumed that a "good product" should sell by itself. Technical quality rather than client's preferences guide the product design. Services around products, such as repair or installation services, are aimed at optimal technical functioning of the supplied product rather than at client satisfaction.

For example, Mercedes Benz in the eighties provided high quality maintenance services but paid little attention to client needs such as the necessity for rapid service or obtaining a replacement car.

Durability of products is not directly linked to client preferences. It is predominantly shaped by the producer's notion of what is solid, durable and reliable.

41

M. Kostecki (ed.) The Durable Use of Consumer Products, 41–49.

The concept of durability which fits into a product-centric strategy is static and focuses on the product rather than performance which, as a last resort, determines the usefulness of the product's durable life.

Cost-Centric Strategy

Cost minimization is given priority over durability. Price and availability are main determinants of success in mass consumption societies. There are few services around the product. Consumer durables don't last. They are expected to be thrown away after a limited use and destroyed or re-cycled. That strategy is encouraged if the producer or consumer do not bear the environmental cost of the product's production, re-take and re-cycling.

For example, until recently, producers of sweet drinks relied extensively on non- recuperable packaging. Recent legislation in Holland, Germany and Denmark encourages the use of refillable bottles (Di Gennaro, Ventimiglia, 1996).

A cost-centric strategy implies that durability is neglected, especially if it is costly to provide. In order to contain the negative environmental impact of cost-centric strategies it is necessary to internalize environmental costs through appropriate legislation.

Sales-Oriented Strategy

The firm puts most energies into hard selling. Given its product concept and production capacity it concentrates on promotion to stimulate more buying. Clients are assumed to resist purchases and have to be coaxed into buying. Producers and distributors stimulate demand by increasing the symbolic obsolescence of their products (e.g. by promoting new fashion). Post-purchase satisfaction is not a high priority and maintenance services are considered as an unavoidable burden.

For example, clothing or sport equipment requires intensive promotion. Product life cycle is accelerated through rapidly changing fashion designs and novelty.

Product durability is not a priority even if it is desired by the client. It may be consciously limited to maximize the sales of new products. Lack of appropriate services and spare parts or their high cost further limit the useful life of products

Client-Oriented Strategy

Durable products are offered when desired and not offered when durability is low among the attributes valued by the targeted clients. The firm offers both hardware and services combined in well-performing systems which contribute to client's value chain and satisfy the firm's business objectives. Product durability is services-based. A new durability and reliability concept emerges and creates new business options.

For example, a company leasing cars, is interested in maximizing performance of a system composed of hardware (car) as well as maintenance and insurance services.

Durability is client-focused. The increased importance of customer services and emphasis on performance of systems composed of material goods and services modify the business view of the useful life of a product. Firms are willing to provide "durability services" because such services may provide a promising area for their profitability and growth.

2. THE SYSTEMIC CHANGE AFFECTING PRODUCT DURABILITY

Strategic response requires an understanding of the turbulence that the firm is likely to experience, meaning the extent to which the firm's environment is changing (Ansoff, 1985). An appraisal of the turbulence affecting product durability in advanced (OECD) countries is summarized in Table 3.1. Let us briefly explain the various concepts and their significance for product durability.

Table 3.1

SYSTEMIC CHANGE AFFECTING A USEFUL LIFE OF CONSUMER GOODS			
PERIOD **FACTOR**	**I** **(1945-65)**	**II** **(1965-90)**	**III** **(1990-2010)**
Dominant nature of economic system	Reconstruction Industrialization	Affluent society	Service economy
Value	"Contained" in products		Determined by performance
Markets for hardware	Captive and naive	Competitive	Saturated
Market scope	National	International	Global
Strategic technology	Mechanics	Computer Tele-communications	Integrated information systems
Standardization and compatibility	Limited	Discouraged to keep captive markets	Open systems are favored
Product life cycle	Moderate	Short	Revised to fit system performance
Consumption	Restrained consumption	Mass consumption	Informed consumer
Environmental concerns	Low	Increasing	High
Dominant factor of success	Technical	Managerial orientation	Client orientation

In the period of economic reconstruction and industrialization (period I) the dominant strategy of the leading industrial firms in the markets for consumer durables were product-centric especially for products in the early stages of their life cycle (e.g. refrigerators, cars, washing machines, TV sets) and sometimes cost-centric when primary needs (e.g. housing) were to be rapidly satisfied by mature products.

Product-centric strategies meant that the technicians responsible for product development and production determined durability according to the traditional standards of their technical profession. The relative importance of consumer's need to possess (rather than use) further encouraged products that appeared solid and durable. Relatively moderate technological change also favored long-lasting goods.

In the affluent society of mass consumption (period II) cost-centric strategies became dominant in the mature markets for consumer durables. Markets became highly competitive and increasingly international (Hoekman, Kostecki, 1995). Product life cycles were progressively shortened to generate constant new demand. The symbolic "in" components of numerous goods such as cars, clothing, sporting equipment, etc., were constantly modified to generate additional demand. The life of durable consumer products was considerably shortened.

Accelerated technological change is rendering numerous existing products inefficient or obsolete. Moreover, technology-dominated product design at times results in product complexity which leans towards what is desired by the consumers (e.g. complexity of washing machines in Europe or H.F. equipment where 80 of the available options is not known by the client) and reduces durability.

A market of second-hand (used) goods is emerging for certain important categories of products such as cars and to a lesser extent, household equipment. However, the markets of used products and services (including marketing services) around them are archaic and of embryonic nature. Moreover, the existing legislation about new products limits certain promising options.

Standardization of spare parts and system compatibility are discouraged to enable monopolistic pricing of maintenance products and services and therefore further limits durability. The proliferation of cost-centric and sales-oriented strategies makes things worse. The mass consumption of throw-away durables as well as the environmental costs of production and recycling contribute to awaking the environmental concern.

The old patterns of producer-consumer relations are breaking down in the service economy creating new challenges and opportunities for product durability. Services have become central in the way that industry was central at the time of the industrial revolution (Giarini, 1994). The industrial revolution did not mean that agriculture ceased to be important. It simply meant that whatever important happened in agriculture, had its origins in industry. Today, whatever important happens in industry has its source in services (R&D, telecommunication, data processing, design, problem-solving, customer services, etc.).

The modern economy value is closely attributed to the performance and utilization of products and services integrated in a system. The quality of performance rather than the quality of output becomes the main criteria of evaluation. The quality of the consumer's experience (including the quality of the producer-consumer relationship) is a critical determinant of business success in the emerging service economy (Giarini,1989, Giarini, Stahel, 1993, Kostecki, 1994).

In a service economy the emphasis is on solving consumer's problems rather than on selling goods and services. Consultative selling puts services at the leading edge of the solution approach, rather than considering them as an afterthought. This means that the producers have to understand specific customer needs, and in response propose specific solution processes. This is largely a service-based approach (Karoutchi, Kostecki, 1994).

Suppliers increasingly offer personalized solutions and results (rather than individual products and services). They have to favor transparency and open systems which maximize clients options of choice. For communication, suppliers have to translate their product specifications into the language of consumer benefits. Such an approach is a categorical imperative not only for service firms, but also for manufacturing companies which increasingly recognize the merits of matching consumer needs with services-based solutions. Numerous traditional manufacturing companies increasingly turn into service companies with a major portion of their profits and growth being generated by services rather than manufacturing activities (e.g. Digital, Schindler AG. IBM).

In modern service economies the traditional consumer-supplier dichotomy is breaking down. Customer and supplier value chains have to be closely connected to achieve the goals of both parties. What matters is not only a product-cash transaction, but a supplier-client relationship where both parties add value. Suppliers have to learn how to establish a profitable "partner-client relationship" (Christopher, Payne and Ballantyne,1991). Partnership among producers is valued, opening new avenues for standardization, compatibility and open systems.

Switching from a product-centric to a consumer-centric organization is for most firms a necessary condition of business survival in such an environment. This creates new options for increasing a useful life of products, where appropriate, through a joint effort of suppliers and clients. The client-oriented strategy is a winning option. Integrated systems optimizing performance and product durability are gaining ground. Such an approach opens new opportunities for redesigning products, rethinking their consumption technology and offering services that contribute to increase useful life of goods. Many questions arise in that context.

What are the major challenges confronting businesses and government policies with respect to product durability? What issues should be better studied and understood to provide guidelines for strategy formulation?

3. THE ROADMAP OF CHALLENGES

What are the critical issues in consumer marketing aimed at extending a useful life of products through increased durability, better re-use, increased intensity in use, etc.?

Product

– *Technical quality "to last"*
How much of it is desired by consumers? What is the cost of alternative improvement strategies? What are the dominant attributes of "durable products" from the consumer's perspective? What is the consumer perception of the attributes of "re-used" or "second-hand" products? What are the benefits of such products from the perspective of the consumers' value-added chain? What strategies of market segmentation should be followed with respect to "durable products"?

– *Services around products*
What mix of services is needed to increase the useful life of products and to optimize a system's performance? How should product design be modified to allow the consumer to take fuller advantage of open systems (e.g. increased system compatibility or standardization of parts)? What organizational changes are required to merge products and services into performing systems with marketing benefits and an increased useful life of products?

– *Risk of extended use*
What are the differences between the perceived risk and the actual risk related to the extended use of products? What are the typologies of such risks and what marketing strategies may be developed to deal with these particular types of risks? What guarantee should be offered to reduce a negative perception of risks resulting from the extended life of products?

Customer Service

– *Building a relationship with the customers*
How may services related to the extended life of products be used to build a relationship with the customers? How can they provide a strategic advantage over foreign-based (lower-cost) competitors? What is the impact of such services on the consumer's image of a trademark, her/his loyalty and mouth-to-mouth communication?

– *Sale*
Are product-durability services useful in identifying consumer needs and in prospecting? In what cases may such services constitute a strategic advantage (i.e one that makes the company sell its products? What type of communication should be used to emphasize the attributes of durability at the time of sale?

– After-sale satisfaction
What is the influence of "durability services" on the after-sale satisfaction, the consumer's perception of a trademark, and brand loyalty? What are the determinant factors of product durability and related services in increasing after-sale satisfaction?

Price

– Durability-cost pricing
What is the best strategy to incorporate the cost of "durability" into a product pricing scheme? How does product durability affect the relationship between price and perceived value? What fraction of a product's value is attributed to durability?

– Pricing and guarantee
What pricing methods are most appropriate to optimize a positive consumer's attitude towards a durable product? What is the impact of guarantee attached to "used products" on the products' perceived value?

– Pricing and client motivation
What is the most satisfactory financial client-producer relationship to maximize product durability? What are the appropriate pricing schemes for optimizing a client's contribution to product durability? How can pricing strategies be used to motivate re-take chains and product re-use? How can government regulation of pricing schemes eliminate externalities which shorten useful life of products?

Communication

– Dealing with anti-durability bias
How can the current communication approach which favors novelty and new products be corrected? What communication strategy is necessary to render durability "in"? What type of synergies may be exploited by durability leaders in private business and by public bodies to support socially beneficial policies of durable goods?

– Consumer benefits
How can the advantages of product durability be explainded? How can the complexity of "durable systems" be communicated to the consumers? What communication approach is the most beneficial in influencing the consumer's perception of risk and certain other attributes of product durability?

– Corporate image and brand image
How can the company's innovative strategy aiming at an increased useful life of products be communicated? What type of image benefits can result for those "durability leaders" who communicate their innovative strategy to the consum-

ers? What is the durability image of "made in" for various countries and how does it affect consumer choice?

– Durability policies
What communication strategy is there for durability policies? What is the most effective pattern of lobbying for "durability legislation" on the part of the business leaders interested in imposing higher durability standards on their competitors?

Distribution

– Distribution and durability concerns
What distribution problems limit product durability and how can one deal with them? What distribution factors encourage product durability?

– Globalization and product durability
What is the relationship between durability services around products (which tend to be local) and the trend towards globalization of consumer products?

– Consumer and distribution
What motivation schemes should be used to stimulate consumer's (prosumer's) contribution in the distribution systems favoring durable products. What type of successful solutions in the area do exist? What innovations may be suggested?

Process

What benchmarks can be found from case studies from a typology of the most successful service processes which encourage the useful life of products? What are some examples of networks and partnership arrangements in that area? What are their driving forces and what are the typical conflicts in the system?

Strategy

What are the future threats and business opportunities in service economy and product durability that include environmental change and strategic implications for durability? What is the strategic response to current trends in consumer preferences? What are the costs and benefits of durability leadership? How does one evaluate costs and benefits of a durability strategy? – a framework for analysis (durability audit).

BIBLIOGRAPHY

ADLER, L. and HLAVACEK, J. "The Relationship between Price and Repair Service for Consumer Durables" in *Journal of Marketing*, vol. 90, 1976, pp. 80-2.

ANSOFF, H. I. (1985) "Strategic Response in a Turbulent Environment" *Handbook of Business Strategy*, Boston: Warren, Gorham & Lamont, pp. 2-18.

BÖRLIN, M., STAHEL W. (1989) *An Economic Strategy of Durability*, Geneva, The Product-Life Institute (memo)

CHRISTOPHER, M. PAYNE A. and BALLANTYNE D. (1991) *Relationship Marketing*, London, Butterworth Heinemann.

DEUTSCH, CHRISTIAN *Abschied von Wegwerfprin zip*, Schaffer Poeschel, 1994.

DI GENNARO, MONICA AND VENTIMIGLIA, PATRICIA (1996) *La durabilité dans l'embalage, mémoire de licence en marketing*, Université de Neuchâtel.

GIARINI, ORIO "The Service Economy: Challenges and Opportunities for Business Firms"in *Marketing Strategies for Services* , M. Kostecki (ed.),Oxford, Pergamon Press, pp. 23-40.

GIARINI, ORIUO and STAHEL, WALTER (1993) *The Limits to Certainty: Facing Risks in the New Service Economy*, Dordrecht, Boston, London, Kluver Academic Publishers.

HOEKMAN, BERNARD, KOSTECKI, MICHAEL (1995) *The Political Economy of the World Trading System*, Oxford, Oxford University Press.

KAROUTCHI, J., KOSTECKI, M. (1994) "Customer Orientation in Business Services: Digital's Solution-Mapping Technique: TOPway". *European Journal of Marketing*, vol.12, no.2 pp. 179-188.

KOSTECKI M. (1994) "Le markeing dans l'economie de service", *Revue Française du Marketing*, no. 149, vol. 4, pp. 25 – 31.

KOTLER, PHILIP (1991) Marketing Management, Englewood Cliffs, Prentice Hall.

STAHEL, WALTER R. (1994) "The Utilization-Focused Service Economy: Resource Efficiency and Product-Life Extension", Allenby, Braden R. (ed.) *The Greening of Industrial Ecosystems*, National Academy of Engineering, National Academy Press, Washington D.C., pp. 178-190.

STAHEL, WALTER and JACKSON, TIM (ed.) (1993) *Durability and Optimal Utilization-Product-Life Extension in the Service Economy*, Stokholm Environment Institute, Lewis Publishers, Boca Raton, Ann Arbor, London.

VANDERMERWE, SANDRA (1994) "Service Network Structures for Consumer-Oriented Strategies", *Marketing Strategies for Services*, M. Kostecki (ed.), Oxford, Pergamon Press, pp. 41- 64.

CHAPTER 4

PRODUCT STEWARDSHIP AND USEFUL LIFE CONCEPTS:
The Challenges for Business in the 21st Century

JAN-OLAF WILLUMS
Director, The World Business Council for Sustainable Development, Geneva

Has *Product Stewardship* brought the production and use of goods and services in better alignment with the goal of sustainable development? Or is there an underlying contradiction between the production-oriented industrial society and the vision of sustainable development that cannot be bridged? This chapter aims at identifying the challenges that industry is faced with in the debate around sustainable production and consumption, and the role of Product Stewardship.

1. PRODUCT STEWARDSHIP AND EXTENDED PRODUCT RESPONSIBILITY

The Product Stewardship concept originated from Dow Chemical in the early 1970's. Since then, many multinational companies have launched "product stewardship" or "product responsibility" programs, including Hewlett-Packard, Intel Corporation, Xerox Corporation and Northern Telecom (WBCSD,1996).

Product Stewardship focuses on "making environmental, health and safety concerns a priority in all phases of a *product's life cycle*, and as a result, lessening the adverse impact of products on human health and the environment" (Flaherty,1996). As outlined in the product responsibility guidelines of companies such as Dow, SC Johnson and 3M, product responsibility begins with research and development, that is, at the point of a product's conception, and extends through product design, manufacture, marketing, distribution, use, recycling and disposal.

Voluntary product stewardship concepts can become a significant factor in the mindset of all of industry if the policy framework is set right. If not, the pioneers in accepting a widened product responsibility may not gain the competitive advantage that an extended view of the product cycle should yield, seen from a global societal viewpoint.

M. Kostecki (ed.) The Durable Use of Consumer Products, 51–55.
© 1998 *Kluwer Academic Publishers. Printed in Great Britain.*

While Product Stewardship emphasizes *voluntary* action, governments can choose to set a complementary framework through the concept of *Extended Product Responsibility* (EPR). EPR also aims at resource conservation and pollution prevention, and similarly to the voluntary stewardship model, advocates a *life cycle* perspective to identify strategic pollution prevention and resource conservation opportunities. The principle of shared responsibility ensures that designers, suppliers, manufacturers, distributors, users, and disposers each take responsibility for the environmental impact of products throughout the entire product life.

While Product Stewardship is voluntary, and thus may not cover all industrial producers (the "free-riders" problem), it is driven by competitive objectives and not only "compliance at minimum cost". It should therefore be more efficient in societal terms. Even if it mainly covers the larger and more visible players, their efforts may be more important as a "demonstration" process with peer pressure effects. This view is taken by the US President's Council for Sustainable Development: "The greater responsibility rests with the actors who have the greatest ability to influence the environmental and energy impacts of the specific production system, depending upon the product's specific characteristics" (US President, 1996).

2. CONSUMPTION AND SUSTAINABLE DEVELOPMENT: A CONTRADICTION IN TERMS?

The critics may raise the more fundamental question:Can consumption be sustainable, or is this a contradiction in terms? Can the production of any goods or services be sustainable? It seems odd that these questions should be high on the agenda of business – to the extent that 48 of the 120 companies of the World Business Council for Sustainable Development (BCSD) joined in a working group to explore in depth how these concerns and challenges would influence business strategies into the 21st century.

The interest was triggered by the Rio Earth Summit. Sustainable production and consumption (SP&C) emerged as a key theme at the Earth Summit in June 1992. Agenda 21, the proposed Program of Action which was adapted by 178 governments at Rio states that "... the major cause of the continued deterioration of the global environment is the unsustainable pattern of consumption and production, particularly in industrial countries, which is a matter of grave concern, aggravating poverty and imbalances" (UNCED, 1992 Agenda 21, Sec. 4.3).

The response, as suggested by the same UN declaration, calls on governments and all stakeholders and especially business, to strive for efficiencies in production and changes in consumption patterns in order to emphasize optimization of resource use and minimization of waste (Agenda 21, Sec. 4.15). Whereas some have equated this with a call for dramatically reduced consumption per capita, it will not solve the global challenge: the rapid trend in economic development outside the OECD countries and the urgency of stemming the tide of poverty fostered by a rapidly increasing population in the Third World, are not served by reducing consumption in the North alone. With the globalization of the world through expanding trade, and the information age creating the "global village" communicating by Internet, the issues of sustainable production and consumption must be solved globally.

3. PRODUCT INNOVATION VERSUS SYSTEMS INNOVATION

The business community generally sought the key to a global solution in innovation and increasing efficiencies. An increasing number of companies realized that they do not need to focus on technological innovation alone (although it makes an important contribution) but also on innovation of the mindset. They understood that by looking at the environment and on developmental challenges from a more constructive conceptual perspective, rather than threat perspective, industry may find unexpected solutions, and discover uncharted opportunities.

The rapidly rising demands of the fast-growing population in many countries are not met by "business as usual". What is needed is a shift of magnitude and of a new dimension – a change by factors, not degrees. A rising number of scientists and technologists are convinced that the way we do things today can be improved significantly, at least by a factor of 4 (von Weizsäcker, 1996). Some believe that one can even go well beyond this factor 4, and have created the "Factor 10 Club". By setting the goals high enough, they rightly say that you create vision and not merely foresight. This in turn requires ways to measure in rough terms the real impact on the environment (Schmidt, Bleek, 1995). Here are the real challenges for the academic community – to help measure corporate efficiency in striving towards sustainable development.

4. ECO-EFFICIENCY AS A NEW BUSINESS STRATEGY

It is easy to understand that the wider business community sees a threat in demands calling for a radically reduced consumption and limited production. Value has, in the past, mainly been generated through a steadily growing demand for goods and services, and a rising purchasing power. Why should the world community ask those countries that are on a rapid economic growth path today to be deprived of the same development?

This is a difficult question to answer, especially as business leaders in many rapidly growing economies today are also more aware of the global implications of an uncontrolled growth than their colleagues in the North were a generation ago. They see the challenges that business leaders have to face in balancing economic growth with environmental stewardship more clearly, and look for creating value rather than single-minded economic growth. Many of the 600 business leaders that have formed the 17 national or regional Business Councils for Sustainable Development are clearly aware of the dilemmas and challenges facing global business as we move into a new century.

One way to meet this challenge is to focus on the opportunities rather than only on the problems. More and more business people realize that unique innovative approaches allow a revision of the industrial process in its totality. This concept of Eco-Efficiency, as promoted by the World Business Council for Sustainable Development, is beginning to unleash creative resources in many of the participating companies. Instead of trying to improve performance, the concept tries to radically change the way we produce.

5. HOW CAN BUSINESS CONTRIBUTE TO SUSTAINABLE PRODUCTION AND CONSUMPTION?

Eco Efficiency is not just "business as usual", but requires a radical shift in attitudes by both business leaders and the whole production process. Eco-efficiency is a *management philosophy*. It encourages business to become more competitive, more innovative, and more environmentally responsible. The pursuit of eco-efficiency does not require companies to abandon all their current practices and systems. It calls for them to adapt these in order to achieve higher levels of economic and environmental performance through conscious improvement. It links environmental excellence with business excellence.

This does involve making some tough choices and decisions. Companies may not only need to examine how they do business but also whether they should continue to produce some of their products. Some companies are seriously considering whether or not the customer of some of their major products really need or want the product, or would rather look for a service that another type of product could be providing in a more eco-efficient way.

These companies are already re-appraising their traditional methods of running their business by *considering the entire life cycle* of their goods and services. This in turn has a direct impact on design and engineering, purchasing and materials management, production, marketing, distribution and waste management. Eco-efficiency means thus that the life-cycle thinking, and thus the basis for product stewardship, is elevated from an engineering discipline to a strategic management concept. This is an important shift that should be fostered and supported by research in the academic community (Willums, 1995).

BIBLIOGRAPHY

FLAHERTY, M. (1996) Making the Link: Sustainable Production and Consumption, Geneva, WBCSD.

SCHMIDT BLEEK, F. (1995) Produktenentwicklung – Nutzen gestalten – Natur schonen, Wien, WIFI Publication no. 270.

US President's Council for Sustainable Development (1996) Final Report, Washington D.C.

VON WEIZSÄCKER (1996) Factor 4, Wuppertal Institut, forthcoming
WILLUMS, JAN-OLAF (1995) Eco-Efficiency and Education. Geneva, EEMA Conference
    Proceedings.

CHAPTER 5

SUSTAINABLE PRODUCT DESIGN

MARTIN CHARTER

Coordinator, The Center for Sustainable Design, UK

The first part of the chapter gives an overview of the concept of sustainable development. Then various definitions of environmentally-conscious product design are examined, with a discussion over the links between the 'Design for Environment' (DfE) or eco-design and Industrial Ecology.

This chapter suggests that 'Sustainable Product Design' (SPD) has a key role to play in the movement towards a more environmentally sustainable form of consumption and production. However, a key issue will be the implications of the addition of the social and ethical dimension alongside the environmental and economic elements of the product design and development process. Ideas relevant to the SPD in the context of service product development are also explored.

1. SUSTAINABLE DEVELOPMENT

"Only by re-thinking some basic assumptions about functions, tastes and lifestyle will we be able to move in any significant way towards a more sustainable way of living" (Mackenzie, 1991).

Movement towards a sustainable future requires vision, education and the of change of attitudes and behavior. The development of the concept of Sustainable Product Design (SPD) will require more awareness amongst senior level management, design managers and designers of systems thinking. It is also necessary to balance the 'quadruple-bottom' line: economic, environmental, ethical and social needs. Ultimately the concept of SPD will require senior level commitment, if resources are going to be allocated. It means, if it is to move from an interesting philosophical concept to something more 'concrete'.

Of particular importance will be the need to design in 'closed-loops' i.e. to remanufacture, re-use, etc. Business firms have to reconsider the product/service relationship (i.e. should the product be bought, rented or leased or should there be some hybrid arrangement). Ultimately, SPD will require designers and design

57

M. Kostecki (ed.) The Durable Use of Consumer Products, 57–68.

managers to approach design briefs in a more holistic and innovative manner.

The balancing of environmental, social and economic needs is the key essence of the sustainability agenda. The term 'sustainable development' became more widespread as a result of the Brundtland Report in 1987, and since then a range of definitions have emerged, primarily with an environmental bias. Sustainable development is now a theme running through national and international environmental policy, but the practical application of the concept is still in its infancy.

> "Development that meets the needs of today without compromising the ability of future generations to meet their own needs" ('Our Common Future', 1987)

The practicalities of the concept of sustainable development are still unfolding. Currently it has a different meaning (frequently controversial) to different people: wealth redistribution from rich to poor nations (intra-generational equity); maintaining the earth so as not to impoverish future generations (inter-generational equity); population control. The fundamental idea, however, is clear: to manage the earth's resources in such a way as to maintain a global carrying capacity which is ecologically sustainable over time, given the continued evolution of technology and maintenance and the enhancement of the 'quality of life'.

The business response to the sustainability agenda is still patchy – even committed and aware organizations are struggling to operationalize the concept. The International Institute for Sustainable Development in Canada has developed a definition from a business perspective:

> "Sustainable development means adopting business strategies and activities that meet the needs of the enterprise and its stakeholders today while protecting, sustaining and enhancing the human and natural resources that will be needed in the future."

This definition recognizes that if firms are to play a part in sustainable development there needs to be the involvement of a range of stakeholders, each of whom are likely to have differing interests. Thus a vision of a more sustainable company will require a multi-stakeholder 'buy-in' and will have significant implications for corporate culture and organizational design.

2. THE BUSINESS RESPONSE TO SUSTAINABLE DEVELOPMENT

A range of issues have heightened business awareness and sensitivity to the environment. These include tougher environmental laws, the advent of the 'green' consumer and the uncertainties surrounding ozone depletion and climate change. A key focus for business was The Earth Summit in 1992 where two key initiatives came together – the Business Council for Sustainable Development (BCSD) and the International Chamber of Commerce's 'Business Charter for Sustainable Development'.

In January 1995, the BCSD merged with the World Industry Council for the Environment (WICE) to form the World Business Council for Sustainable Development (WBCSD) representing the interests of many of the world's largest companies. Sustainable consumption and 'Design for Environment' issues are agenda items for WBCSD.

But, where do we stand now? Translating sustainability down to the level of the product is primarily about moving away from 'end-of-pipe' technologies to clean or 'green' designs. A recent study by Ashridge Management Center indicated that in the UK, as compared to other parts of Europe, there appears to be a lack of interaction between environmental managers and new product development and marketing. This finding was reinforced by the Institute of Environmental Management's survey in the UK which indicated that product planning and marketing were at the bottom of most environmental manager's responsibilities.

Table 5.1

BUSINESS AREAS OF FUNCTIONS THAT ENVIRONMENTAL MANAGERS HAVE MOST CONTACT WITH									
	Total	Germany	Netherlands	US	UK	Chemicals	Energy	Manufacturing	Consumer products
Production	2.3	2.6	2.0	2.5	2.3	2.1	2.4	2.4	2.5
Research and development	2.0	2.2	2.1	2.0	1.9	2.1	2.3	1.9	1.9
Marketing/Sales	1.7	1.8	2.0	1.9	1.2	1.3	2.3	1.5	1.8
New product development	2.0	2.0	2.3	2.3	1.5	1.9	1.6	2.3	2.0
Transportation/ Distribution	1.4	1.4	1.5	1.5	1.4	1.4	2.1	1.3	1.0
Human Resources	1.3	1.3	1.5	1.5	1.4	1.4	2.1	1.3	1.0
Public Relations	2.2	1.9	2.1	2.5	2.1	2.9	2.3	1.6	1.9
Finance/Accounting	1.3	1.1	1.4	1.3	1.5	1.5	1.6	1.0	1.1
Corporate Development/Planning	1.8	1.4	1.9	1.9	1.9	2.1	2.2	1.5	1.3
Information Systems	1.4	1.3	1.9	1.4	1.3	1.5	1.4	1.4	1.5
Training	2.1	1.9	2.3	1.6	2.5	2.0	2.0	2.3	2.0
Legal Advisers	2.3	2.0	2.1	2.4	2.5	2.4	2.4	2.5	1.8
Health and Safety	2.4	2.4	2.4	1.9	2.4	2.6	2.9	2.5	1.9

The respondents were asked to rank their contact on a 3 point scale in which: 1 = little contact with, 2 = some contact with, 3 = a lot of contact with

Source: The European Environmental Executive, James and Stewart, Ashridge 1995

It appears that environmental managers often have to use the 'stick' of likely threats of non-action on environmental issues in relation to marketing, rather than marketing 'seeing' the opportunities. This possibly reflects an increasing risk aversion. Environmentally-driven innovation (eco-innovation) needs to be stimulated and facilitated by environmental managers, with those responsible for design taking a key role in the process.

Figure 5.2 The Environmental Manager: Non-environmental Responsibilities

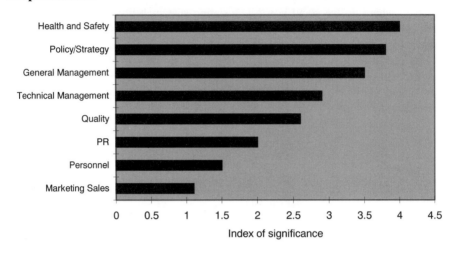

Figure 5.3 The Environmental Manager: Principal Environmental Responsibilities

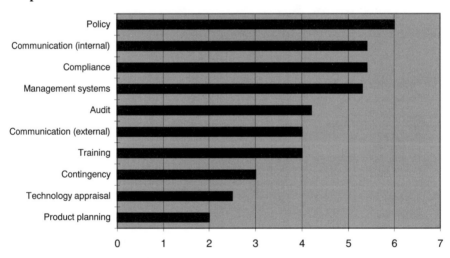

3. PRODUCT DESIGN AND THE ENVIRONMENT

All products and services have an environmental impact. 'Tangible' products are based on materials which have been derived from 'the environment', to which they will return in some form. At the start of a product's life, design and development pre-determine the product or services' environmental impact. This influence extends beyond the product's useful life, as all material will usually have to be converted or transferred, before it is returned to the environment.

Product designers have historically neglected the life of a product after it has served its functional purpose. The increased costs of waste disposal and the implications of producer responsibility and product take-back legislation are starting to change this, particularly in electronics and packaging industries. A major objective of eco-design or 'design for the environment' (DfE) is to design products with the aim of minimizing life cycle impacts and costs. Solutions are to extend the useful product life through reuse and re-manufacture, and design for 'end of life', which concentrates on the safe disposability and re-introduction of materials into the market.

Over the last ten to fifteen years various concepts, systems and approaches have been developed to advance the goal of producing products with less impact on the environmental (with services often being forgotten). However, the concept of Sustainable Product Design, which goes beyond eco-design or DfE, is a new and emerging debate.

Broadly, there are two generalized definitions relating to environmentally-conscious product design: specialist and broad-based.

Table 5.2

ENVIRONMENTAL ISSUES AND DESIGN: EXISTING DEFINITIONS	
Specialist	Design for energy efficiency
	Design for disassembly
	Design for recyclability
	Design for refurbishment
	Design for maintainability
Broad based	Green Design
	Ecodesign
	Responsible Design
	Life-cycle Design
	Design for Environment
	Designing for 'X'

Specific definitions:

Many of the early successes in environmental product improvements were a result of companies concentrating on specific issues such as 'design for refurbishment', 'design for disassembly', and 'design for recycling'.

Broad-based definitions

However, some companies are experimenting with more systematic, broad-based approaches and this has spawned a range of definitions. Essentially, eco-design appears to be a European definition and 'design for environment', the North American definition. Both approaches are being primarily driven by environmental managers rather than the marketing and design functions.

4. ECO-DESIGN

Eco-design is the development – or re-development – of products, while keeping in mind the environment. Other terminology includes 'Environmentally Friendly Design' and 'Green Design', which all aim for the same outcome: to reduce the environmental impact of manufactured products.

> "Eco-design aims to minimize the product's overall environmental influence by incorporating environmental criteria related to the whole life cycle of the product in the development process. Eco-design therefore goes beyond the correction of just one or two negative environmental aspects of a product. It considers the product as a whole. The objective may either be to redesign a product in order to improve its environmental influence, or to design a totally new product with inherently better environmental performance".(Dr. JC van Weenen, Chairman of the UNEP-Working Group on Sustainable Product Development).

5. DESIGN FOR ENVIRONMENT (DfE)

To assure that companies continue to identify and profit from new opportunities and keep ahead of increasingly tough pressures, leading companies such as Xerox and Phillips are beginning to practice a more systems-orientated design approach: design for environment (DfE).

DfE is sometimes viewed as a module of the existing design system known as 'Design for X', where 'X' is the desired product characteristic, although it can be integrated into any design process.

> "DfE designates a practice by which environmental considerations are integrated into product and process engineering design procedures.. DfE practices are meant to develop environmentally compatible products and processes while maintaining product price/performance and quality standards." (B.Allenby and A.Fullerton, 1991)

DfE practices are designed to be comprehensive, multi-disciplinary approaches for integrating environmental concerns and constraints into product and process design procedures. Implementing DfE is likely to require major changes in the existing organizational culture of many firms.

6. MANAGING ECO-DESIGN OR DfE

Another key issue is how you manage the eco-design or DfE process within the firm. This is a particularly complex issue for multi-product / multi-market /

multinational companies – as the 'stage' of evolution of the eco-design or DfE strategy will be dependent on a range of internal and external issues.

One may be in a position where a firm may have an eco-design or DfE infrastructure without it being systematically organized or explicitly stated. There may be a corporate motherhood statement about product stewardship in an environmental policy without any particular understanding as to the practicalities of the statement. Subsidiary A, may have an initial strategy; subsidiary B, may be aware of the issues, but may not have tackled them and, subsidiary C may think it is something to do with environmentalists.

What is the present reality? Two studies from Decision Focus and The Centre for Sustainable Design have indicated similar results in the electronics industry.

- The environmental manager, rather than the designer, often appears to be driving the eco-design or DfE process.
- 'Producer responsibility' is perceived to be an increasingly important issue and drives the eco-design or DfE.
- There is a lack of information and training particularly for product designers, many who have had no form of environmental training.
- There is a lack of framework to manage and measure the effectiveness of the eco-design or DfE process.

A majority of companies already starting to focus on eco-design or DfE are struggling with how to start the process, and how to understand the eco-impact of existing new products. This occurs prior to understanding the eco-impact of new products development. Inclusion of wider social and ethical issues are not on the agenda and are unlikely until (a) more mature eco-design or DfE systems are developed or (b) more coherent models of 'the shape' of a more Sustainable Enterprise arise.

Below are some suggested guidelines for those starting the process.

The Eco-Design or DfE Process: a checklist
I.   Senior-level commitment
II.   Develop an eco-design champion
III.   Create an eco-design budget
IV.   Complete an eco review of existing produces/services
V.   Develop an eco checklist for new product development
VI.   Establish an eco-design philosophy/policy
VII.   Establish qualified eco-design objectives
     A.   products overall
     B.   product groups
     C.   specific products (brands)
VIII. Establish an eco-design strategy
     how you are going to achieve the objective
IX.   Establish an eco-design programme
     A.   budgets
     B.   responsibilities

  C.   time-scales
X.   Develop a long-term response to Sustainable Product Design (SPD).

The eco-design strategy must reflect the organization, its cultures, products and markets. Its 'shape' will be different for each organization.

Eco-design or DfE principles:
Translating specific eco-designs or DfE principles to the level of product design will differ from company to company but common themes are likely to include:

Material Selection
• minimize toxic chemical content
• incorporate recycled and recyclable materials
• use more durable materials
• reduce material use

Product Impacts
• reduce process wastes
• reduce energy consumption
• reduce use of toxic chemicals

Product Use
• increase energy efficiency
• reduce product emissions and waste
• minimize packaging

Design for Recycling and Reuse
• incorporate recyclable materials
• ensure easy disassembly
• reduce materials diversity
• label parts
• simplify products (for example, number of parts)
• standardize material types

Extension of the Useful Life of Products and Components
• design for remanufacture
• design for upgrade
• make parts accessible to facilitate maintenance and repairs
• incorporate reconditioned parts or subassemblies

Design for End of Life
• safe disposal

Several of the above themes also concern the optimal use of products.

7. INDUSTRIAL ECOLOGY

Over the last five years industrial ecology has evolved around the idea "that there is no waste in nature" i.e. that all waste is a potential input for another organization, process or system. DfE is a method to operationalize industrial ecology at the product level. Designing products to achieve zero or minimal emissions will mean that product systems should attempt to mimic nature; therefore, product designers will have to be aware of a wider range of issues than previously.

Producing beer or plastic is a complex issue but linking industries into clusters is an even higher level of complexity. Therefore, the philosophy is about moving beyond the single product, single costing and core strategy approach where one company makes one product and doesn't go beyond its field. It is about collaboration, partnerships and inter-linkages.

"...the traditional model of industrial activity, in which individual manufacturing processes take in raw materials and generate products to be sold plus waste to be disposed of, should be transformed into a more integrated model: an industrial ecosystem. In such a system the consumption of energy and materials is optimized and the effluents of one process, whether they are spent catalysts from petroleum refining, fly and bottom ash from electric power generation or discarded plastic containers from consumer products, serve as the raw material for another process" (Frosch and Gallopoulos, 1989).

Beyond the year 2000, we are likely to see more industries clustering together to develop new solutions. This process will bring industries closer together so that boundaries and demarcations may become increasingly blurred. A competitive edge will be converted into a sustainable advantage, with sustainable advantage generated by groups of companies, virtual organizations or groups of industries which have developed complimentary, supportive, multi-disciplinary teams to solve eco-problems. Therefore the main shift in business thinking will be a movement from the single company, single product thinking to a more integrated holistic vision.

8. SUSTAINABLE PRODUCT DESIGN

SPD has a crucial role to play as an intermediary stage between eco-design or DfE, industrial ecology and the vision of sustainable development. The key issue will the addition of social and ethical dimensions to the debate, when people are struggling with balancing environmental and economic aspects. Many of the implications are, as yet, unclear. It will not just be about product attributes but it will be about the way the firm is managed, the way suppliers and their suppliers are managed, and the role that the firm plays in society, both on a local and global scale.

Social and ethical issues need to be added into eco-design or DfE to take it towards Sustainable Product Design (SPD). The concept should be essentially applicable whether for assembling vehicles for space travel or for growing potatoes for local consumption in Kenya.

Figure 5.3 Sustainable Product Design

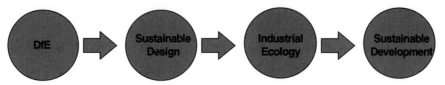

The overall aim of the Sustainable Enterprise should be to deliver products/services that function, have achieved the required quality as well as service levels and balance the other three elements of the 'quadruple bottom line'. The underlying aim is to deliver the appropriate return to stakeholders, including reasonable profit. SPD is essentially about balancing the 'quadruple bottom-line': environment, economic, ethical, and social needs.

Some of the key elements and considerations in relation to SPD are likely to be:

• Needs versus wants
• Functionality
• Longevity
• Balancing environmental, economic, ethical and social factors
• Human health and toxicity issues
• Generating eco-solutions, solving eco-problems
• Reduced and more efficient use of resources: eco-efficiency
• Working with nature, not against it
• Systems-orientated
• Innovative
• Holistic
• Stakeholder-orientated
• Minimizing environmental impact across the product's life cycle
• Aiming for zero emissions

The Center for Sustainable Design has developed a working definition of Sustainable Product Design:

> "SPD is a design management practice which aims to balance environmental, social, ethical and economic needs. SPD acknowledges the need to develop innovative product and service concepts which minimize environmental and social impact throughout the life cycle. SPD is a systems-orientated approach that recognizes the need to form broader stakeholder relationships and partnerships. The aim is to produce zero emissions."(M. Charter and A. Chick, The Center for Sustainable Design).

9. SERVICE PRODUCT DEVELOPMENT

SPD does not only relate to 'tangible' products but it should also be taken into consideration in service product development. The coffee shop in an airport has various elements that make up *the service*. These include the coffee itself, cups, brewing, storage, etc. There are also other factors such as 'what if' the coffee is consumed and the cups are disposed of in bins in the forecourt. There are social and ethical impacts, as well as more obviously environmental impacts to *the service* provision. For example, Starbucks Coffee in the US mention on their paper cups:

> "Caring for those who grow our coffee – Healthy beginnings in Indonesia: with our support CARE has provided over 35,000 women and their infants with access to health services, immunization and nutrition education in southern Indonesia. Please join Starbucks in support of CARE by calling 1-800 521-CARE".

Clearly, there are a range of human issues involved in the growing of coffee: fair wages, working conditions, use of pesticides, etc.. But equally these issues relate to complex organizations with complex products. For example, many electronics companies are moving the manufacture of components to the Far East and the same issues are true irrespectively of the complexity of the tasks undertaken.

10. SYSTEMS-FOCUS

A key issue is whether it is feasible to develop a sustainable product or service in an unsustainable system. It is therefore essential that the responsible product/service designer takes account of the long-term conditions that will enable a more sustainable system. He should also design exemplary, best practice products or design products that minimize unsustainable impacts: environmentally, socially and ethically.

Therefore, should the designer be developing and using socially responsible life-cycle analysis (SRLCA) in particular, focusing on 'consumption systems'? For example, are you designing a kettle, a water heating device or a device for heating water for drinks / cooking? This thinking then leads us into the relationships between the kettle and the tea/coffee growers / distributors / packagers / shippers and many of the social and ethical issues discussed above. Should the designer be looking at designing to minimize the 'sustainability' impact of 'the kitchen experience' throughout the life-cycle?

11. CONCLUSION

Design has an important role to play in producing more sustainable solutions to the existing, as well as to new product and service problems. The issue of optimal life span of consumer durables and other aspects of their optimal use is seen in a larger context of sustainable consumption and production. If this is to be maximized then there is a need to gain senior management commitment to the process and facilitate discussion between environmental, marketing and design management, as well as a broader range of external stakeholders. In addition, there is a need to develop better frameworks to manage the eco-design or DfE process, and to provide better training, information and tools for designers. Designers will need to develop a broader understanding of the interaction between environmental and social systems, and look for 'closed-loop' opportunities to extend existing products and re-use waste. A key issue will be educating business people and particularly marketers about the opportunities arising from the sustainability agenda. If SPD is to move from the 'think tank' to 'real life', it will be essential to understand the organizational reality of the concept and generate business benefits in relation to the development of products, services and hybrids. To achieve balanced 'quadruple bottom-line' solutions to sustainability's complex, evolving, changing problems or opportunities, managers and designers will need to develop the ability to 'think', 'to think creatively' and to 'think out of the box'! Clearly it is not 'business as usual' and new structures, skills and systems will have to be developed.

BIBLIOGRAPHY

ALLENBY, B. and FULLERTON, A. (1991) "Design for Environment: a new strategy for environmental management", *Pollution Prevention Review no. 4.*

Brundtland Report (1987) *Our Common Future,* Report of the World Commission on Environment and Development (WCED), Oxford, Oxford University Press.

CHARTER, MARTIN (1995) 'Interview with Gunter Pauli, Zero Emissions Research Initiative (ZERI)', *The Green Management Letter*, Euromanagement, Eindhoven: The Netherlands, May.

CHARTER, MARTIN and CHICK, ANNE (1995), 'Towards Sustainable Product Design', *Towards Sustainable Design' Conference*, The Center for Sustainable Design, Farnham: UK, July.

CHARTER, MARTIN (1996) 'Sustainable Product Design', *The Green Management Letter*, Euromanagement, Eindhoven, The Netherlands, March .

DILLON, PATRICIA (1994) *Design for Environment*, Washington DC., World Industry Council for the Environment (WICE).

FIKSEL, JOSEPH (1995) 'Design for Environment' – unpublished survey results, *Decision Focus*, Mount View: US, October.

FROSCH, ROBERT and GALLOPOULOS (1989) 'Industrial Ecology: Minimizing the Impact of Industrial Waste' *Physics Today*, November

MACKENZIE DOROTHY (1991) *Green Design: Design for the Environment*, Lawrence King: US

SHERWIN, CHRIS and CHARTER, MARTIN (1996) *Environment, Design and Electronics: Survey Results,* The Center for Sustainable Design, Farnham: UK, June.

CHAPTER 6

PRODUCT RESPONSIBILITY IN THE US ELECTRONICS INDUSTRY[1]

PATRICIA S. DILLON
The Gordon Institute at Tufts University, USA

1. INTRODUCTION

Electronics firms are subject to a proliferation of international environmental policies and standards that go beyond traditional concerns about manufacturing process wastes and releases to impact corporate management practices, product design and marketability, and post-consumer product disposal. Their suppliers and customers are increasingly sensitive to environmental issues such as energy efficiency, material use (e.g., recycled content, ozone depleting substances concerns), and environmentally-sound product disposal and recycling, motivating electronics firms to manufacture and supply appropriate products and services.

The market for electronic products is highly competitive. Indeed, global competitiveness today hinges on delivering products that meet customer's price and performance preferences, while improving the life cycle and environmental performance of products. Customers may desire more environmentally-sensitive products and services, but for the most part, they are not willing to pay for this added benefit[2]. What sells, both with customers and internal management, is environmental benefit translated into business or product performance. The bottom line is, therefore, still the same. The challenge, or opportunity, is finding solutions that merge business opportunity with environmental improvement.

As examined in this chapter, product life cycle management[3] offers opportunities to converge environmental and business performance objectives: for example, to lower the cost of doing business for a manufacturer as well as for its

---

[1] The material presented in this chapter was partially funded by the US Environmental Protection Agency, Office of Solid Waste and Emergency Response through Grant No CX 824366-01 to the University of Tennessee, Center for Clean Technologies.

[2] This point is confirmed by the companies participating in the research project, as well as by colleagues from other electronics firms.

[3] These programs are also referred to as product stewardship or extended product responsibility.

69

M. Kostecki (ed.) The Durable Use of Consumer Products, 69–81.
© *1998 Kluwer Academic Publishers. Printed in Great Britain.*

customers, or to increase customer satisfaction by offering products and services that meet the environmental performance needs of customers. This chapter demonstrates how customer needs, expectations and regulatory trends are translated into product, process or service features at three electronics companies – Compaq Computer Corporation, Hewlett-Packard Company, and Northern Telecom.

Each of the companies has developed a systematic approach to the life cycle management of its products across the corporation, building on efforts in the 1980s to control and reduce manufacturing emissions and waste. These companies are now extending their influence up and down the supply chain, beginning with product design and supplier relations, and continuing to the end of the product's useful life, to improve both economic and environmental performance of products and services.

This chapter examines selected corporate strategies for achieving the dual goals of environment and business at these global electronics companies, including product life extension through upgradeable designs and asset management, design for reuse and recycling, new packaging concepts, energy efficiency, and supplier management.

2. DESIGN FOR ENVIRONMENT AT COMPAQ COMPUTER CORPORATION

"We believe that striving for exemplary environmental performance is essential to sustaining market leadership." Compaq 1994 Summary Annual Report

World-wide competitive pressures have led Compaq Computer Corporation, the world's largest supplier of desktop and portable personal computers, to redefine the boundary of its product life cycle. In earlier years, Compaq considered its job done when the product left manufacturing and was sold in the marketplace. The introduction of a 3 year warranty extended Compaq ownership concerns through service and support. With the advent of "take-back" legislation in Europe, Compaq's view of the product life cycle was stretched all the way to the end of its product's life.

This paradigm shift created a new mandate for design. The ability to cost-effectively service and repair the product, as well as recycle the product at the end of life, became an integral part of the competitiveness equation.

In 1994, Compaq completed a comprehensive environmental design guideline. The design guide promotes the adoption of a life-cycle perspective in the design of products, and specifically addresses the following issues:
- Material selection, focusing on recyclability
- Design for disassembly
- Packaging materials
- Energy conservation
- Design for reuse and upgradeability

Table 6.1 highlights some design parameters within each category.

Table 6.1

EXAMPLES OF COMPAQ DESIGN GUIDELINES

• Packaging
    • Minimum 35% recycled content
    • No heavy metals in packaging inks
    • 100% Kraft paperboard, no bleach
    • Use of recyclable materials only
• Plastics
    • Use only recyclable thermoplastics
    • Consolidate plastic types
    • Use ISO markings to identify resin type and exact blend
    • No paint finishes
    • Labels: molded in or use same resin type as housing
• Disassembly and Recycling
    • Use of standard screw heads
    • Design modular components
    • Minimize number of parts
• Energy Conservation
    • Comply with Energy Star standards
• Design for Reuse
    • User upgradeability
• Use of industry standard architecture

Compaq finds synergy between design for environment (DFE) and other priority design objectives, namely design for manufacturability and design for serviceability. For example, fewer parts simplify manufacturing while facilitating recycling. Similarly, easy disassembly facilitates the servicing, upgrading and recycling of equipment as well.

3. EASY UPGRADEABILITY

One of the most promising "reuse and recycling" opportunities for Compaq is upgradeable products. Product upgrade features help avoid early obsolescence and increase the product life by facilitating the replacement of electronic components, while avoiding the unnecessary disposal of mechanical parts, such as the plastic housing, power supply and metal chassis, which do not impact product functionality. At the same time, Compaq can reduce its costs and the customers costs, while increasing its competitiveness.

For example, a customer who purchased a 486/33 MHz computer with 4 megabytes of RAM will have trouble running Windows 95. Rather than discarding the old computer and buying a new Pentium-based computer, a user can attain similar results by upgrading the microprocessor to a Pentium and adding additional RAM. The added bonus is that the upgrade is a fraction of the cost of a new computer (for example, the upgrade costs approximately $300 compared to $2000 for a Pentium-based product).

While any PC can be upgraded, if you have the technical knowledge and are willing to replace the motherboard or manually de-solder the microprocessor chip and potentially end up with a mess (PC Magazine, 1996), Compaq's designs are truly "upgradeable" by the average user without the use of specialized tools and the risk of damaging your computer. This is accomplished through the use of alternative technologies for mounting components and easily accessible subassemblies. In Compaq's recent ProLinea[R] and Deskpro[R] models, a user can easily upgrade the entire motherboard, the microprocessor, or the memory and easily access the hard drive and expansion slots to replace or add new features.

One technology that enables easy upgrades is the ZIF (zero insertion force) socket that holds the microprocessor in place on the motherboard. This socket replaces the traditional solder mounting, which is considered a semi-permanent connection technology. The ZIF socket uses a tension bar to hold the microprocessor and force a connection. This technology allows the user to easily remove and replace the old microprocessor and install updated or faster technology, simply by unlatching and re-latching the bar.

From an environmental vantage point, upgradeable products conserve resources. For the most part, however, this is not critical to the purchasing decisions of customers, who are concerned predominantly about costs and product features. For Compaq and its customers, the upgradeable PC is important from another angle. It lowers the lifetime cost of computer ownership, a growing concern to customers as technological obsolescence occurs at an ever increasing rate.

In this regard, Compaq's marketing literature extols the virtues of its upgradeable product:

> "Needs change, goals change, and people change. The good news is, a Deskpro computer can change every bit as quickly. It opens without any special tools. The system board slides out, making it easy to upgrade the processor or add extra RAM. The PCI expansion slots are easily accessed. And the drive cage swings out to make hard drive upgrades painless... With the task of upgrading a PC reduced to minutes, you can allocate your time to more lucrative pursuits." (Compaq Deskpro product literature, 1995.).

Upgradeable products also lower the costs of servicing products, for those customers who do not want to do it themselves. In addition, due to efforts to design upgradeable products, Compaq computers are easier to disassemble. Components such as microprocessors, hard drives, and memory are also pulled out easily and undamaged, which facilitates resale and reuse opportunities.

While upgradeability has several advantages, both environmental and economic, it does have its limitations. The biggest limitation is technological change. If the basic architecture of the computer or its components changes, for example, upgrades might not be an option. So, for a computer coming on the market today with upgrade features, it is unclear how long the current technology will be compatible with future generations.

4. Product Life Cycle Management at Nortel

"Nortel sees sound environmental management as a key contributor to customer and shareholder value. The company continually seeks to exceed mere compliance and to minimize resource consumption, waste and adverse environmental impact, limited only by technological and economic viability." Nortel's Corporate Environmental Policy

Nortel is convinced that environmental excellence is good business. They realized this first with chlorofluorocarbon elimination. Nortel saved four times their one million dollar initial investment over three years. Similarly, a business case on investment in environmentally-related programs developed in 1995 to support the pursuit of Nortel's environmental targets revealed an impressive 1:4 ratio of investment to return.

With its Product Life Cycle Management (PLCM) program, Nortel believes they can save money for customers and themselves, increase customer loyalty, and create value for their customers through efficient use of resources, such as reusable packaging, longer life products, and asset recycling. Nortel also believes that a segment of the marketplace will choose environmentally-preferable products. Indeed, some large telephone operating companies, such as British Telecom and Telia (Swedish) Telecom, are querying suppliers about the use of hazardous materials in products and product recyclability.

Nortel approaches its product life cycle management program strategically. Consistent with corporate operating principles, the program aims to create customer value. Customer value takes many shapes, including: lower lifetime costs of product ownership through resource efficiency; partnerships with customers to improve their environmental performance; and value-added recycling of products at the end of life. PLCM also strengthens strategic alliances with suppliers, which are of growing importance to Nortel's overall business strategy.

The mandate of the PLCM program is to improve the environmental performance of the corporation through changes in all stages of the product life cycle design, supply management, manufacturing, marketing, distribution, and product disposal. Activities underway include, for example:

- working upstream with suppliers to redefine responsibilities and requirements;
- redesigning products to eliminate toxic materials and improve resource efficiency;
- improving manufacturing operations through energy efficiency and research into the use of VOC-free fluxes and lead-free solders;
- implementing packaging improvements that minimize wastes; and
- reducing environmental impacts at the product's end of life through recycling initiatives.

5. Energy Efficiency: A Major Target

To lower product costs, Nortel strives to root out inefficiencies and waste in the design, delivery, and use of its products. Energy efficiency is a major target.

Study after study conducted by Nortel identifies energy efficiency as a major leverage point for environmental improvement of products and processes. More energy-efficient products translate directly into lower costs for customers, since energy is a major cost of operating telecommunications equipment.

Energy efficiency is also a major environmental objective of Compaq and Hewlett Packard. According to EPA projections, with the power management features activated on the desktops and monitors Compaq shipped in 1995 alone, the estimated worldwide energy savings could be as much as $60 million dollars. For the environment, this means a reduction in fuel use and power plant emissions, translating into reduced CO_2 pollution equal to the emissions from 150,000 automobiles.

Hewlett-Packard offers more than 100 product models that meet or exceed US EPA Energy Star criteria, including 100 percent of its printers, plotters, facsimiles, 486-based PCs, and PC display monitors. Given the proliferation of Energy Star products on the market, however, Hewlett Packard does not consider the Energy Star logo to be a market differentiator. Conversely, the absence of the logo is seen as a competitive disadvantage: for example, President Clinton signed an Executive Order in 1993 requiring federal agencies to purchase only computers and printers that meet Energy Star requirements.

6. SUPPLY MANAGEMENT AND CHEMICAL USE REDUCTION

Nortel is investigating new business opportunities in supply management to help the environment and lower costs. In an effort designed to reduce chemical use, Nortel is embarking on an innovative business strategy with its chemical suppliers. In a pilot project at one of Nortel's Ottawa, Ontario sites, Nortel is initiating a new business relationship with its main chemical supplier. Under this new relationship both Nortel and its chemical supplier will have a joint incentive to reduce chemical use.

The hallmark of such a relationship is a change in the once competitive nature of the manufacturer/supplier relationship. Instead of the supplier seeking profit by encouraging Nortel to use more chemicals, under a "shared savings" relationship, Nortel and its chemical supplier will work together to minimize chemical use. In its long-term contract, Nortel purchases the services of the supplier for a fixed fee, rather than purchasing the chemicals themselves. In this way, Nortel removes the financial incentive of the supplier to sell more chemicals. In this new relationship, the supplier is responsible not only for supplying the needed chemicals, but also for providing a services such as chemical process expertise and chemical management, storage and disposal. As a result, the supplier has the incentive to help Nortel minimize chemical use by introducing innovations, searching for alternatives to hazardous chemicals, suggesting more efficient chemical processes, and delivering only the quantity of chemicals needed.

Such a supply management relationship allows Nortel to concentrate on what it knows best – network solutions in the telecommunications industry – while leaving the chemicals to the experts. The ultimate impact is reduced chemical use and costs and increased quality in products and processes due to the leveraging of outside expertise. By inviting suppliers into such long-term business relationships, Nortel is developing an innovative solution that can help the environment and makes good business sense.

7. EXTENDING PRODUCT LIFE THROUGH DESIGN

A modular philosophy was adopted for Nortel's new Vista telephone models, called Power Touch in the U.S.. The new model allows the customer to upgrade the unit without buying a new one and scrapping the old one. The principle driver behind the design was to create "user value" by leveraging the customer's initial investment through a flexible and upgradeable design. The new model is designed in two parts – a standard base with basic telephony features and an upgradeable slide-in module that can add features such as caller ID, call waiting, a larger screen size or a better graphics display. The base holds its design for a longer period of time, while the module can be replaced to provide the latest features at half the cost of replacing the telephone. This new design minimizes product obsolescence and reduces the volume of product headed for recycling or disposal.

Long life products are not new to the telecommunications industry, where equipment is typically in the field for 15-20 years. Nortel's Meridian office systems introduced in the 1970s were "backwards compatible", which means that even in the 1990s a customer can easily upgrade and expand to provide enhanced communication capabilities without replacing the entire system. While the Meridian system was unique at the time, the architecture of new systems is increasingly modular in design to enhance upgradeability and expansion and to allow "plug'n'play" with any manufacturer's equipment.

8. ASSET RECYCLING

Nortel operates three recycling facilities in North America and one in the United Kingdom with a mission "to provide entrepreneurial solutions and services for the valued recovery of materials and surplus assets while demonstrating environmental leadership". To accomplish this mission, the reclamation operation provides Nortel divisions and customers with a full range of asset disposal and recycling services, from equipment test and refurbish to resale of useable components to recovery of precious and non-precious metals and plastics. The operation has a good profit margin with approximately 85 to 90 percent of the revenues being returned to business units, and even to customers where applicable, while 10 to 15 percent cover operating costs.

Nortel's reclamation operations date back to the 1970s, when they opened a facility in Barrie, Ontario to provide an equipment recycling service to Bell

Canada, a major customer. The facility primarily processed metal-based products, particularly copper, to achieve maximum separation and recovery value for Bell Canada. The origin of Nortel's US reclamation facility in Durham, North Carolina was quite different; it started in 1990 as a central collection and disposal point for Nortel surplus assets such as desks and other non-telecommunications office equipment. Today, however, the Durham facility handles mostly telecommunications equipment and is the central return point for Nortel products coming back from the field.

In the US and Canada, the reclamation operation processes 50 million pounds of equipment annually, including central office switches, private branch exchanges, cable and components from excess and obsolete inventory. About 50 percent of the equipment processed is Nortel's own equipment excess and obsolete inventory. Trade-ins and removal from customer sites account for the other 50 percent, although Nortel is actively trying to expand services to commercial customers and suppliers. In the United Kingdom, for example, Nortel negotiated with British Telecom to begin taking back some older varieties of PBX equipment for reuse and recycle. In addition, Nortel is working with other European distributors to develop tailored Product Take Back (PTB) services to suit distributor and market conditions.

Over 90 percent of the equipment processed at the facilities (by weight) is recovered for reuse or recycling. Product and component reuse and resale (for example, circuit boards, memory chips, line cards) account for approximately 50 percent of revenues, playing a greater role today than in the past. Three years ago at the Barrie, Ontario facility over three-quarters of the equipment was electro-mechanical or copper-based cable, which was granulated or shredded to recover metals. In contrast, today more than half of the equipment is processed for reuse and resale. There are two reasons for this. First, the value in the recovery of raw materials is declining due to a reduction in the precious metals content of the products processed at the facility. Second, technology is moving at a faster pace, which results in a greater rate of equipment turn over. While the equipment might be obsolete by some customer's standards, it may still be functional or contain reusable parts.

The amount of material going to landfill has decreased from 10 percent to 4 percent over the past several years as a result of a zero landfill program aimed at reducing solid waste disposal costs. (The goal for 1998 is only 2 percent to landfill.) The zero landfill program identified alternative disposal options and reuse opportunities for materials going to landfills. One waste stream targeted was pallets. The solution in this case was to route the pallets back to the business units for reuse, rather than disposing of them. In addition to saving landfill costs, this program saves the business units approximately $70 on the purchase of each new pallet (after inspection and redistribution costs). As a result of the zero landfill program, disposal costs at the Durham facility were reduced approximately 90 percent from 1992 to 1994.

9. ASSET MANAGEMENT AND RECYCLING AT HEWLETT PACKARD COMPANY[4]

Managing the end of life of electronic equipment provides multiple business opportunities for Hewlett Packard (HP), from improved customer service and sourcing of spare parts to new revenue streams in some cases. The company's two equipment recovery operations in the U.S. are strategically located within the HP organization to reflect their mission. The Hardware Recycling Organization (HRO) is part of the Support Materials Organization (SMO), which is responsible for worldwide distribution and repair service material. In contrast, the home of the asset management group servicing the Technical Computer Business Unit, also known as Alternative Inventory Solutions, is within the marketing group.

The primary mission of the Hardware Recycling Organization (HRO), located in California, is to recover useful service parts through the disassembly and refurbishment of HP and non-HP excess equipment and parts. HRO also serves as one of HP's recycling hubs. Equipment and parts that are not suitable for service are routed to environmentally-responsible, non-competitive recovery channels.

Salvaging parts from used equipment allows HP to improve its service levels; in particular, it increases parts availability while lowering costs. Indeed, the origins of the HRO operation lie here. In 1987, HP found it difficult and expensive to obtain new service parts for some printers. In its search for solutions, the service organization found tear down of used equipment and subsequent refurbishment of parts to be a cheaper and more reliable source of service parts. HRO could fill an order for spare parts in 2 weeks time, in comparison to over 6 months for some new parts. HRO now stocks the service supply pipeline, resulting in an immediate turn around for service parts. Stocking service parts using the HRO organization also frees up HP's manufacturing capacity, allowing production units to concentrate on manufacturing new products. In addition, for some older technologies which are no longer in production, the recovery of service parts from used equipment is the only option, and therefore, is vital to keeping equipment in service.

The HRO facility processes 9000 tons of equipment annually with a total recycling rate of over 99 percent, including some incineration with energy recovery. Less than 1 percent of product goes to landfill. Sixty percent of the equipment processed at the facility comes from HP divisions (e.g., internal equipment, excess inventory), while de-installation from customer sites and HP's service organization account for 25 percent and 15 percent, respectively.

At the facility, incoming product lots are weighed and unpacked. Product numbers are entered into a computer system and any service parts identified. The products are then routed to either disassembly for removal of service parts or reclamation. Equipment that is not utilized for service is diverted to non-competitive recovery channels, including component resale and material recy-

---

[4] Hewlett Packard has an extensive product stewardship program that encompasses supplier management, design for environment, as well as asset management, the focus of this section

cling. Of the equipment processed, the disposition of products breaks down as follows:

- 70 percent reclamation, which includes pulling integrated circuits and material recycling of precious metals, plastics, nonferrous metals, and CRT glass;
- 18 percent resale of components and parts, such as disc drives, fans, motors.
- 12 percent recovery of parts for use in HP's service organization. Service parts designated for recovery include, for example: electronic assemblies, boards, drives, and monitors.

In the past, the HRO program was passive; they waited for equipment to come to them. This is changing into a more active program, a program that deliberately pulls products from markets into the HP recycling system in order to recover valuable service parts. For example, in late 1994, HP's marketing department initiated a tradeup program for LaserJets with a dual goal. An obvious goal was to increase the sale of new LaserJets; an additional driver was added to increase the supply of spare parts to the service organization and to lower service costs. HP will also buy back equipment that they are interested in for service parts, although they offer no formal product take-back program.

The biggest problem materials for the recycling organization are plastics and cathode ray tubes. HP is beginning to find solutions for plastics, now that the company is looking at plastics recycling from a financial perspective. One year ago, HP was sorting all plastics, despite a lack of markets for the material. The company then shifted its focus to recover only those plastics that were in market demand, and in particular, plastics that were in demand by HP. HRO started with ABS, which represents 12 percent of the waste stream. HP worked closely with a resin supplier to develop a recycling solution and infrastructure, which allows closed-loop recycling of ABS. Using the ABS model, HP plans on tackling other plastics, in particular, polystyrene and polycarbonate, which together with ABS, account for 80 percent of the recoverable plastics stream.

For HP's HRO organization, the bottom line is that the recovery of service parts is very profitable, while the unit strives to break-even on its recycling activities. Historically, the largest revenue generators have been chip recovery, precious metals, and resale of disk drives, fans and motors. However, these markets are volatile (as demonstrated by the plummet in the DRAM market in mid-1996), impacting the economics of electronics recycling. In addition, CRTs and plastics recycling are financial drains, although ABS recycling is reaching a break-even to slightly positive cash flow.

10. ASSET RECYCLING OF WORKSTATIONS

The HP Technical Computer Business Unit (TCBU), which manufactures workstations and other high-end computer systems, operates its own recycling organization from its headquarters in Massachusetts. Like the HRO organization, this recycling operation, also known as Alternative Inventory Solutions (AIS), has strategic importance to the company. The program:

- provides alternative sources of equipment and service parts to HP;
- ensures that equipment does not enter the gray market;
- recovers maximum value from equipment, without damaging new product sales; and
- ensures proper disposal of equipment.

A workstation, or Unix server, has greater value when it enters the marketplace and when it leaves the marketplace, compared to a PC or printer. For this reason, HP is able to recoup "significant" savings and revenues (after expenses) from this operation. Over 70 percent of the equipment and subassemblies processed by AIS is returned to HP for reuse or resale, while only 30 percent goes to third parties for recycling. Reuse and resale opportunities include, for example:

- product remanufacture, where systems are upgraded to incorporate design changes or features introduced since the product's inception (e.g., CPU board upgrade). These systems are tested to ensure that they meet HP quality standards;
- recovery and refurbishment of service parts for HP internal use (e.g., boards, disc drives, cables.);
- sale of commodity items (e.g., disc drives, monitors, integrated circuits) to secondary markets;

HP is trying to increase its sale of remanufactured equipment. Such equipment may fill an existing customers' expansion needs or target new markets. New markets are targeted for strategic purposes. For example, HP seeks entry into new geographic and vertical markets, where potential customers may not be able to afford the latest technology (e.g., developing countries, educational institutions). Used product sales create current revenue streams, while increasing HP's presence in the market and competitive edge for future sales of new product. Used equipment is also offered for sale to HP partners, such as software developers, to create goodwill and strengthen alliances. Whether reselling remanufactured equipment or parts, however, HP is careful not to compete with new product sales or HP's service organization.

11. NEW PACKAGING CONCEPTS REDUCE WASTE, SAVE MONEY

For Nortel, Compaq and Hewlett-Packard, packaging was an obvious target for waste reduction, as legislation worldwide focused attention on this waste stream and disposal costs skyrocketed. As a result, technological innovations, new packaging concepts, and common sense solutions are springing up, leading to significant cost savings. At Nortel, for example:

- Standardization and redesign of distribution packaging saves approximately $5 million annually. These savings were achieved by standardizing, and thus reducing the number of packaging configurations. The resultant reduction in the number of box configurations led to a greater reuse of boxes, the need for less storage space and sorting, and fewer boxes purchased.
- Shipping switching products in assembled mode, rather than packaging and

shipping components separately for on-site assembly, saves an additional $5 million annually. The "plugs in place" shipping method requires less packaging, and reduces installation time.

- Nortel designed a new "clamshell" packaging system for shipping circuit boards that eliminates cardboard and foam waste, and is reusable. The packaging is also designed to improve handling and storage for customers. The clear plastic allows customers to scan product bar codes without opening the packaging and risking damage to the product. The nesting and stacking feature of the clamshell also saves space on the production floor.

One innovative solution developed in HP's workstation division requires 30 percent less packaging because protective packaging is built into the product itself, instead of being wrapped around it. The new HP Packaging Assembly Concept (PAC) replaces the metal chassis with expanded polypropylene (EPP) foam. The foam chassis cushions sensitive electronic parts during shipping, while reducing the number of mechanical parts needed to hold parts in position. The foam chassis has an added benefit of reducing product development time, since prototypes require less preparation and assembly time with the easy to mold foam.

Hewlett-Packard's chemical analysis business adopted the innovative E-PAC technology in its new 1100 Series HPLC systems. This new packaging design resulted in major costs savings in assembly and disassembly, since fewer parts and no assembly tools are needed. For example, the new product design resulted in:

- a 70 percent reduction in mechanical housing parts;
- a 95 percent reduction in screw joints;
- a 70 percent reduction in assembly time; and
- a 90 percent reduction in product disassembly time compared to previous models.

EPP foam can also be 100 percent recycled into its source material polypropylene (Huber and Berndt, 1996).

12. CONCLUSIONS

There are good business reasons for product life cycle management or product stewardship initiatives. Indeed, the companies taking part in this research emphasized that "if it doesn't make economic sense, it is not going to happen." The examples highlighted in this case demonstrate the convergence of environmental and business performance objectives, for example:

- Upgradeable designs can slow product obsolescence, increase customer loyalty, lower cost of product ownership, and improve product serviceability.
- Designing products with reuse and recycling in mind can lead to lower manufacturing costs and improved manufacturability due to parts consolidation and reduction in material variety, for example.
- Energy efficient products reduce operating costs.

- Extending product life through asset management strategies may improve the service function, lower disposal costs, create new revenue streams, and introduce products to new markets.

Successful implementation of most of these initiatives is highly contextual, subject to a myriad of product and market variables that must be sorted out on a company-by-company, product-by-product basis. This is particularly true for product recovery and recycling, where product technology, configuration, components, and material composition influence end-of-life opportunities and value. The economics of product recycling is determined further by recycling.

BIBLIOGRAPHY

PC Magazine (1996) Computer Buyer's Guide, p. 42
Compaq Deskpro product literature, 1995.
HUBER, LUDWIG and MANFRED BERNDT (1996) , "Squaring Technical Performance with Environmental Needs," *Today's Chemist at Work*, March.

CHAPTER 7

KODAK'S PRODUCT OPTIMIZATION PROGRAM

HANS H. VAN TEFFELEN
Environmental Affairs Manager, Eastman Kodak Co.

1. KODAK'S MOTIVATION

Eastman Kodak started the new copier division, called Office Imaging or OI, in the early 1980's in France, the UK, Germany and the Benelux as a new challenge in the imaging industry. In 1982 and 83 more countries followed after Kodak got more experience in Europe. Today, Kodak's copier divisions are present in all European countries, a number of countries in the middle East and in some African countries.

The company established an organization with marketing, distribution and service under the same roof as the existing Kodak organizations, many of them established since the beginning of this century. The main objective for Kodak's worldwide management was to strengthen the company's position as an Imaging company in new and different markets and to contribute to the firm's earnings.

In this very competitive market, Kodak identified itself as a high volume copier supplier. In the first years, the company offered only rental products to its customers. To offer rental or lease was very common in this business. Today, Kodak is offering many high speed copiers for high to very high volumes primarily for central reproduction and copy shops, a range of mid volume copiers for office use and color copiers.

Kodak's major challenge is, and always has been, to keep the products installed as long as possible. One of the best ways to do this is through strong *after sales* support. Kodak's Field Service Division consists of highly educated and well-trained service engineers, spread out over the countries, as well as product specialists and spare parts support.

Kodak also felt that product operators and casual users needed support and a good understanding on how to operate the copiers and how to optimize the available features. With the launch of the first copier, the company also announced the concept of the customer support representative.

The after-sales support is an integral part of the copier division, essential for

83

M. Kostecki (ed.) The Durable Use of Consumer Products, 83–88.
© *1998 Kluwer Academic Publishers. Printed in Great Britain.*

the success of the division, for the performance of the products, to keep a high level of customer satisfaction and is the only guarantee that the products' performance is in accordance with the product specifications up to the last day of its life.

There will be a day when the customer decides to have some new or other equipment. This could be because the customer requirements have been changed, that he/she wants to have the latest "state of the art" products or is not happy with the current product. Then the question that comes up is what to do with the old product.

Disposal and or landfill could not be what Kodak, as an environmentally conscious company, wanted to see. In addition, the products generally still had an economic value and were in good shape because of the work done by the Field Service Engineers.

2. OPTIONS

Based on and in response to market studies, Kodak made a strategic decision to offer re-manufactured copiers in addition to new high productivity copiers with outstanding image quality. The re-manufacturing organization was established in 1983 as part of Kodak's Copier Manufacturing in Muhlhausen, Germany.

Kodak has the following manufacturing processes in place:

- *Newly manufactured*
  - new but some parts are previously used.
- *Factory produced new model*
  - based on re-manufacturing and conversion.
- *Re-manufactured*
  - back to manufacturing plant for complete overhaul.
- *Refurbishing*
  - performed in local workshop. Also based on strict guidelines for past performance and number of copies produced.

In order to be re-manufactured, the products have to satisfy certain criteria:

- market potential exists,
- products are good,
- products have been well maintained,
- high quality and low cost re-manufacturing,
- technical performance is as good as new.

After an extensive re-manufacturing, where the products have been disassembled, cleaned, critical parts replaced, performance improved, modifications installed and new or painted covers added, they are sold again to the same or new customers. The life span of the copiers is extended in that way for another 5-7 years or even more.

3. RE-MANUFACTURING PROCESS

To illustrate the re-manufacturing process let us consider the case of two models: the Kodak Ektaprint 225 and the Kodak Ektaprint 235.

The process starts with an Evaluation, based on a physical check and the service history. The service log stays with the copier during its entire life. Management will make a decision whether or not to re-manufacture the copier based on certain criteria, including age, copies made, etc.. In the case that the copier will not be re-manufactured, other options are at our disposal (these will be explained later).

After the evaluation, the copier will be disassembled and the main sub-assemblies are sent to specialized engineering teams for cleaning, parts replacement and testing. The cleaning of the main body and sub-assemblies will not be done with chemicals but with water. Then, step by step, the copier will be assembled again.

After the assembly has been completed, safety and performance tests will be run in order to make sure that the copiers meet the performance and other specifications. New or repainted panels will be added and after a final touch-up, the copiers will be packed, shipped to distribution and will be on their way to new customers.

The key here is that the re-manufacturing capacity is in line with the sales forecast. A flexible, cross-trained work force closely cooperating with Manufacturing is essential for a successful operation.

4. RE-MANUFACTURING ORGANIZATION

The clean and lean organization under the management of Mrs. Angelika Theissen handles many copiers every year.

What has been described before for the Kodak Ektaprint 225 and 235 applies also to the other high volume models 200 and 300 and the mid-volume copiers K 90 and 95 (the so called ECO series). Re-manufacturing is all done in Kodak's plant in Muhlhausen, 4 kilometers south of Stuttgart. Similar facilities have been also established in:

• Rochester, New York (Worldwide Headquarters),
• Tijuana/Guadalajara, Mexico and
• Ostrov, the Czech Republic.

At the Ostrov plant, Kodak re-manufactures all accessories, such as sorters and finishers as well as the mid-volume models (Ektaprint copier K 90 and K95 ECO series).

5. FACTORY PRODUCED NEW MODEL

Kodak's copiers are designed in such a way that they could also be converted into other models with added features as part of the re-manufacturing process. Kodak calls this a Factory Produced New Model (FPNM).

Some very successful programs are the re-manufacturing and conversion of the Ektaprint 235 into the Ektaprint 2085 with an environmental kit and later into the ImageSource 85 where Kodak added major image quality improvements and energy reduction features and the Ektaprint 300 into Ektaprint 3100 also with Energy reduction and other features requested by the customers.

Table 7.1

OVERVIEW OF RE-MANUFACTURING AND PRODUCT CONVERSIONS	
KODAK Ektaprint 160/165	⇒re-manufacturing
KODAK Ektaprint 200	⇒re-manufacturing ⇒re-man. and converted into KODAK Ektaprint 220
KODAK Ektaprint 225	⇒re-manufacturing
KODAK Ektaprint 235	⇒re-manufacturing ⇒re-man. and converted into KODAK Ektaprint 2085
KODAK Ektaprint 2085	⇒re-man. and converted into KODAK ImageSource 85
KODAK 1570/1575	⇒re-manufactured and converted into 1580 ⇒re-man. and converted into KODAK ImageSource 70
KODAK Ektaprint 300	⇒re-manufacturing ⇒re-man. and converted into KODAK Ektaprint 3100
KODAK Ektaprint 90/95	⇒re-manufacturing

The assembly process for some of the models is similar to that of the newly built products and takes place in the same assembly line. All the products mentioned are offered to Kodak's customers with the same service and marketing support as the new products. This concept is well accepted by most of Kodak's customers with the exception of some governments and the European Union. They accept only new products.

6. PARTS RECOVERY

Sometimes it is decided not to re-manufacture a particular copier because there is no market for it or for any other reason. Such equipment goes through the process of parts recovery.

Many parts are designed for a time frame much longer than the life of the copiers. Parts that can be used for field service, manufacturing or re-manufacturing are cleaned, repaired, tested and sent to the Central European Parts Organization in Stuttgart. These parts will be offered to customers at a reduced price. That means that there are benefits for the environment as well as for the customers and the supplier.

Kodak's plant in Ostrov is specialized in reclaiming or salvaging parts. Other parts of the products are disassembled and the materials recycled.

7. LOCAL RECYCLING

Recycling is also an important program in most European countries. Products at the end of their life cycle are disassembled and the materials recycled, or the energy recovered by certified companies. Such an approach allows Kodak to avoid additional handling and transportation.

In Kodak's product development organization, the material selection is the key to success and is linked to the options available at the end of the life cycle. Life Cycle Analyses is an essential tool for the designers. Kodak is also implementing the Design For Environment (DfE) as a way to reduce waste and impact on the environment (see chapter 5). DfE has been fully implemented in Kodak's plant in Germany.

8. OTHER ENVIRONMENTAL ACTIVITIES

For many years, Kodak, as a photographic products supplier, is active in the protection of the environment, particularly in the area of Film processing. The company has established a European Wide Chemical collection program for Photographic Chemicals and Silver recovery through our Chemical plant in Kirkby in the UK.

Kodak also has a worldwide agreement with all camera manufacturers on the collection of single-use cameras. The cameras can be re-used several times.

George Eastman, founder of the Eastman Kodak Company, developed a number of strategies a century ago, which the company still applies to its product offerings. One of his slogans, "You push the button and we do the rest", was developed for the very popular and successful, Box photo cameras. Mr. Eastman's rule also applies today to the office imaging organization. The customer should be able to use the products and shouldn't have to be concerned about all the technicalities.

That is one of the reasons why Kodak has implemented a toner bottle collection program. These plastic bottles are recycled or incinerated with heat recovery.

Even though Kodak's packaging materials do not contain any hazardous materials and could be disposed of locally, the company has implemented a packaging collection program for our high and mid volume copiers. This is done for two particular reasons:
1. economic reasons, and
2. environmental reasons

Kodak's high volume packaging is re-used a number of times, which implies a reduction in the use of natural resources and a cost saving for the company.

9. CONCLUSION

Product life extension at Kodak is a must in order to:
- reduce the impact on the environment;
- limit the use of natural resources and
- avoid high cost for disposal.

That approach is part of Kodak's overall marketing and environmental strategy. The above product optimization program, in order to be effective, has to begin with the design of products.

The re-manufacturing process can only be successful when it is done in the most efficient way to keep the cost at a reasonable level. Kodak offers re-manufactured products with the same reliability as newly build products, but at very competitive prices. Product reliability is a key factor in order to keep the customers' confidence and to keep a competitive edge.

Governments should be made aware that the reuse of products must be stimulated not just by talking to the industry but also as part of the government's own purchasing strategies. This is something that should be changed as soon as possible.

CHAPTER 8

RANK XEROX PRODUCT STEWARDSHIP

IRINA MASLENNIKOVA
Environmental Specialist, Rank Xerox Ltd.

Ever since 1956, when Rank Xerox being in the vanguard of the industry, launched the first office photocopier, the company recognized the environmental effects of its business, either directly because of manufacturing, or through the supply chain and customer operations.

1. RANK XEROX PRODUCT STEWARDSHIP

By 1995, the twin goals of environment and business benefits had been variously and repeatedly proven by Rank Xerox. Behind these are the company's concept of Product Stewardship which has created major step changes in corporate philosophy and continue to drive its environmental performance. Product Stewardship (Figure 8.1) maintains a focus on every stage of a product's life cycle: development and design, procurement of parts and raw materials, manufacturing operations, delivery, customer use and service, recovery from customer premises at the end of life, re-manufacturing, reprocessing of parts and recycling of materials.

Once Rank Xerox became aware of the opportunities in Product Stewardship implementation, this approach no longer applied to the product *per se*, but to the business cycle of the entire company.

2. DESIGN FOR ENVIRONMENT

The interpretation of Product Stewardship is based on Design for Environment (DfE). The Rank Xerox DFE approach includes the following interrelated programs:

M. Kostecki (ed.) The Durable Use of Consumer Products, 89–96.
© 1998 Kluwer Academic Publishers. Printed in Great Britain.

- Multiple lives   - Reduced material mix   - Energy efficiency
- Durability   - Life cycle assessment   - EH&S standards
- Serviceability   - Life cycle costing   - Disassembly
- Parts commonality   - Customer requirements   - Material recycling

Figure 8.1 Design for Environment

In practice DfE requires program managers to develop an environmental plan for each product which focuses on environmental impacts at every stage of the product life cycle. This process embraces the selection of a minimal number of durable materials, well suited for re-use and reprocessing; rigorous inspection for durability, quality and reliability; standardization and labeling of parts with re-manufacturing codes and recycling symbols. Under this, the increasing numbers of components in equipment become interchangeable, compatible and continue their useful lives through generations of Rank Xerox equipment (Figure 8.2).

Figure 8.2 Rank Xerox Product Family Development in 10 Years (1984–1994)

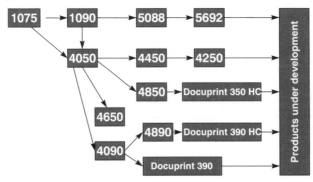

3. WASTE MINIMIZATION

Waste minimization, which represents another umbrella framework of Rank Xerox Product Stewardship, is being driven by the implementation of the Rank Xerox 3Rs policy – Reduce, Reuse and Recycle. This programme covers every stage of Rank Xerox product life and leads the company towards the achievement of its corporate environmental strategic goal.

Waste Free Products include:
* Equipment which consume minimum energy and supplies and is delivered just-in-time
* Returnable and reusable packaging
* Machines which can be remanufactured
* Spares which can be reprocessed
* Waste-free document management solutions.

Waste-Free facilities encompasse all Rank Xerox locations from the design departments through manufacturing sites to the local sales offices.

Considering the context of Product Durability, it is worthwhile to see how the main Product Stewardship umbrella frameworks, described above, have been applied to Rank Xerox equipment and packaging. Those innovative programs have had specific marketing implications and have developed new types of partnership of Rank Xerox with its customers and suppliers.

4. RE-MANUFACTURING STRATEGY

Re-manufacturing strategy, pioneered by Rank Xerox since the late 1980-s, can be regarded as a corporate response to the issue of product and parts durability without compromising the needs of technological innovation.

In 1993 the Asset Management Center was established in Venray (Netherlands). Currently, Asset Recovery employs 350 people in Venray and Mitchealdean (the UK.) with an equivalent turnover of over £100 million per annum. Nearly 2/3 of machines reaching the end of their life with customers are recovered by Rank Xerox and sent to Asset Recovery Operations Units. Of these, 75% of machines (60,000 in 1995) are remanufactured (Figure 8.3) and the remainder is reprocessed (Figure 8.4) and recycled.

Re-manufacturing operations are regarded by Rank Xerox as both a business opportunity and a route to resource conservation: in 1995 raw materials cost savings through AROs were over £ 50 mln (Figure 4.3.); landfill was reduced by over 7000 tons a year (£ 300,000 of saving).

Rank Xerox re-manufacturing operations provide office products with fully guaranteed 'as new' performance – the same people, assembly lines and testing equipment and three years "Total Satisfaction Guarantee" are used both for remanufactured and newly manufactured machines. Figure 8.6 shows that the default rate of Rank Xerox remanufactured equipment is insignificant and quite close to the newly manufactured machine rate.

Figure 8.3   Remanufacturing Machine Throughput

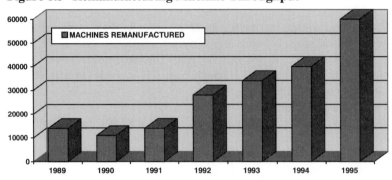

Figure 8.4   Reprocessed Component Throughput

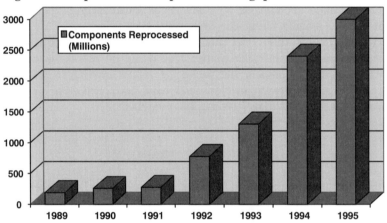

Figure 8.5   Raw Material Cost Savings

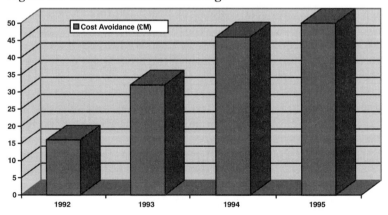

Figure 8.6 Remanufactured and Newly Manufactured Product Quality

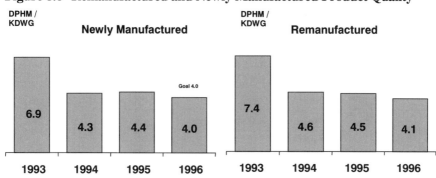

Marketing has always been an important component of the Rank Xerox re-manufacturing strategy: at the beginning the company had to sell customers on the idea that remanufactured machines are just as reliable as newly manufactured ones. In 1993, customer showcases in Western Europe increased customer awareness of the benefits of remanufactured products and highlighted Rank Xerox's positive environmental approach. In 1995, customer demand for remanufactured machines exceeded the forecast by 50%, which, for Rank Xerox, shows that its strategy has been recognized and remanufactured products no longer perceived as "second-hand" (Figure 8.7). Nowadays, Rank Xerox's challenge is to increase the return rate of end-of life products to provide a reliable supply for Asset Recovery Units by embracing remote operating companies and indirect distribution channels.

Figure 8.7 Rank Xerox Remanufactured Equipment: Market Perception

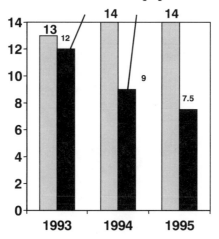

Retaining and regaining Rank Xerox ownership of its products supports the principle of extended producer responsibility and drives further development and implementation of DfE principles within the company. In 1997 Rank Xerox announces its first Waste-Free Product with full re-manufacturing, reprocessing and recycling capability. Every product after that is designed to be waste-free. In the last few years the Rank Xerox re-manufacturing initiative has been emulated by its major competitors which demonstrate the impact it has had on the market-place.

5. RANK XEROX PACKAGING PROGRAMS

5.1. Worldwide Supplier Packaging Standard

In 1990 the Xerox Corporation introduced Worldwide Supplier Packaging Standard 88P311. This major shift was driven by 3Rs principles and resulted in the following main changes:
- 2 standard reusable Euro-pallets were introduced to replace 25 pallet styles, used before;
- 8 standard reusable boxes, modular to the above pallets, to replace 8,000 sent by suppliers;
- Packaging reuse centers were established in the UK, the Netherlands, and the US;
- Bar-coded labels were introduced to improve material tracking;
- Internal packaging was reduced to minimize waste;

The result was $2.1 million savings mostly through re-use of packaging, minimization on packaging waste and just-in-time delivery (Figure 8.8).

Figure 8.8 Rank Xerok Supplier Packaging Cycle

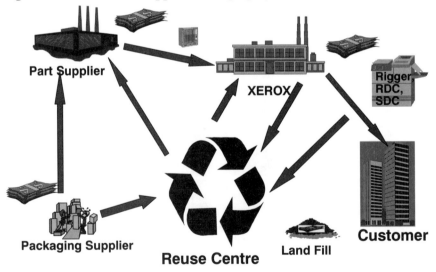

5.2. Packaging Free Products

Since 1991 Rank Xerox has continued its drive to improve and reduce the packaging of its products and in 1994 introduced "Packaging Free Products". The programme is closely associated with re-manufacturing strategy and end-of-life product take-back and is based on the use of two types of returnable and reusable totes: a wooden tote for small desktops and a steel tote for larger machines. The totes have an extensible and collapsible design to accommodate past, present (90%) and future equipment, which is now developed with tote design taken into consideration. The Tote Pool, to which the totes are returned after the total cycle (Manufacturing → Product delivery → Recovery of end-of-life product → Re-manufacturing) is the key point of the whole process and acts as the preferred supplier to manufacturing operations. Similarly to Rank Xerox products, totes can be remanufactured to "as new" status.

Rank Xerox believes that the Packaging Free Products program is a major leap forward for the environment and would encourage other manufacturers to follow its example. This is also a good business – in 1995 Rank Xerox cumulative cost savings realized from the implementation of 'packaging-free' products, packaging reduction and re-use initiatives reached over £3.2 mln (Figure 8.9).

Figure 8.9 Rank Xerox Packaging Savings

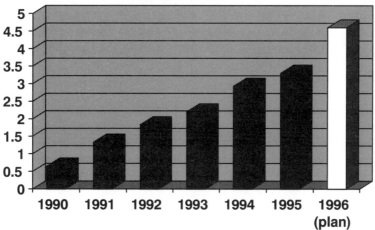

6. THE DOCUMENT COMPANY RANK XEROX

Rank Xerox is now defining its role as The Document Company, moving away from the image of "manufacturer" and "seller" toward that of a document management solutions provider. The company sees a clear synergy between its waste minimization programs, i.e. "Waste Free Office" and move to electronic transmission, storage and manipulation of documents, associated with the most efficient and responsible use of office equipment and consumables. Rank Xerox equipment, with the new generation of energy efficient and paper saving multi-functional devices supports this concept and enables Rank Xerox to pilot new Waste Free Office initiatives in its offices for further communication to the customers.

Rank Xerox achieved BS 7750 certification of its UK factory in Mitcheldean in 1995 and Asset Recycling Unit in Venray in 1996 and is planning to gain EMAS certifications for these sites until the end of 1996. Rank Xerox's first Environmental Performance Report was published in November 1995. In July 1996 Rank Xerox won the European Better Environmental Award For Industry (EBEAFI) as a major external recognition of its waste reduction programs.

CHAPTER 9

PRODUCT STEWARDSHIP: THE CASE OF DIGITAL EQUIPMENT CORPORATION

RICHARD MERLOT

Corporate Program Manager, Digital

There has been an increased interest in and attention to the EHS (Environmental, Health & Safety) impact of products over the past several years. Issues relating to the safety and environmental repercussions of products including end-of-life product take-back, toxic content, design for upgradability, design for disassembly/recovery, recycling, reusability, energy efficiency, packaging, and others, are becoming more important in marketing and sales of information technology products and services. These elements are not only the subject of existing and emerging regulations, but also of increasing interest to customers due to an increased awareness of EHS issues. Additionally, market requirements are being defined in this area with the emergence of a variety of 'eco-label' schemes, e.g. Blue Angel, government procurement guidelines, and self-certification programs. This chapter provides an overview of the components of Product Stewardship at Digital and gives some examples on specific products.

1. WHAT IS PRODUCT STEWARDSHIP?

There are many ideas about what product stewardship is, depending on the context. Digital uses the following definition: working to minimize product impact on environment, health and safety (EHS), throughout the entire life-cycle, while maintaining product price/cost, performance and quality standards. This definition reflects the importance of the essential relationship between EHS and other business aspects of products.

Product Stewardship is a guiding principle which starts before the design phase, continuing during manufacturing, product use, service, end-of-life and final disposition of the product. Product Stewardship allows Digital to balance business objectives with its commitment to health, safety and the environment.

M. Kostecki (ed.) The Durable Use of Consumer Products, 97–104.
© 1998 Kluwer Academic Publishers. Printed in Great Britain.

1.1 Design for Environment (DfE)

At the core of Digital's Product Stewardship are the principles of Design for Environment. Digital believes that responsible Product Stewardship begins with adequate planning at the earliest stage of the product design. This is when a choice between various design options can still be made. The result is a range of products that meets customer, market and legal requirements related to the environment and to user comfort and safety aspects.

Figure 9.1 Extending the First Useful Life

Quality
Reliability
Repairability
Robustness

Upgradability
Modularity
Industry standard
Easy to upgrade

"Classic" design
Style, colour
Never out-of-fashion

Digital is a recognized leader in Product Stewardship. Last year, the US Environmental Protection Agency selected Digital as a Leader in the '1995 EPA Environmental Leadership Program' based on our Design for Environment, Health and Safety program. As part of the EPA Environmental Leadership program, Digital will develop a Design for Environment, Health and Safety guidance manual to assist other companies interested in incorporating environment, health and safety design principles into their product development process. Digital is also planning to assist selected suppliers in their environment, health and safety design efforts. This work will be developed and implemented in collaboration with Massachusetts Institute of Technology (MIT), Environmental Protection Agency (EPA), and the state of Massachusetts Department of Environmental Protection.

1.2. Design for Upgradability

Most customers are interested in extending the life of the computer they are using. Easy upgradability features of products allow customers to upgrade memory, storage, and often even the CPU (Central Processor Unit) without having to replace the entire CPU box.

For example, the Celebris XL Pentium includes a daughter card upgrade feature to allow customers to upgrade easily to higher performance processors (Intel's Pentium Processor, Intel's Pentium Pro-processor, and Digital's Alpha) as their business needs change.

For OEM (Original Equipment Manufacturers) customers, Digital has developed a line of products with durability and upgradability in mind. The systems are custom-built from 'DMCC' (Digital Modular Computing Components). This modular approach allows customers to adjust the performance of their computers to their future needs. Using a range of modular, industry standard designed components, the systems can be upgraded from Intel platform Pentium 75Mhz to high performance Alpha 300Mhz platform and beyond using the same enclosure, backplane and I/O modules.

The result is an extended depreciation schedule for the Digital customer and reduced need to dispose of obsolete computers.

Figure 9.2 Second Useful Life

Take-Back Program

Refurbishment Facilities

Second-hand Market Development

As Good As New

Design for Recycling

As customers replace older personal computers with newer models, they are increasingly concerned with proper disposal of the obsolete systems. One of Digital's solutions to this problem is to ensure that those features which facilitate recycling are integrated into the design phase of the product. Digital's Design for Recycling principles optimize the potential for product re-use, materials recovery, and recycling at the end of the products life. For example, materials used in Digital Desktop PC's are kept to a minimum. Products are designed for easy disassembly, and material combinations that hamper the recycling process or affect proper disposal are avoided. By incorporating recycling techniques into product design, Digital ensures an easier, less costly, and more efficient recycling of product.

Figure 9.3   Recycling Materials > 97.3%

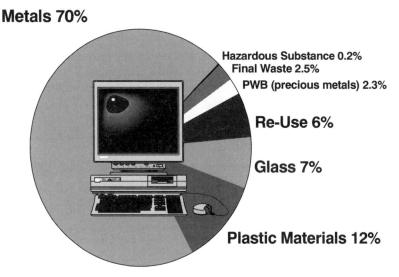

Design for Disassembly

A critical measure of a product's recyclability is the ease with which it can be taken apart. Separating the product into its numerous components is the first step of the re-marketing or recycling process. Digital incorporates a variety of design features, for example: connecting dissimilar materials by joints that are easily separated and the use of fasteners that are easily removed using common standard tools. By designing products so that they are easy to disassemble, Digital reduces costs associated with product recycling. This in turn increases the incentive for recyclers to accept the product from customers at the end of its useful life and reduces the end-user cost of environmentally safe disposition. An additional advantage of design for disassembly is the minimization of material contamination during the recycling process, which can result from the use of glues and adhesives.

Identification of Components and Materials

Identification of components and materials is another important design feature increasing the recyclability of products. Major plastic components are marked in accordance with International Organization for Standardization (ISO) requirements. Providing information to the recyclers about the product composition, components and materials, is an important condition for maximizing reusability and recycling. Digital is very actively participating in the development of « a set of recycling-relevant data to the entity handling the product at the end of its useful life », under the ECMA TC38 (European Computer Manufacturing Association-Technical Committee 38).

2. HAZARDOUS & REGULATED MATERIALS

Increasingly, customers inquire about the materials and substances used in Digital Products. The government has started to regulate product content by prohibiting some substances or limiting its use and marketing. Digital is committed to protect the environment and provide safety to users. That is why Digital carefully monitors scientific information and government regulations on materials used in our products.

Digital works to avoid using potentially harmful substances in its products and has adopted a policy covering the use of regulated materials. For example : plastics used in Digital designed products contain no lead or cadmium ; mercury is not used in connectors or in other electronic components ; and Digital aims at avoiding the use of plastics containing materials that could potentially be damaging to the environment when incinerated. In addition to responsible management of materials in the product itself, Digital also practices pollution prevention during the manufacturing process. Through materials use reduction, the responsible selection of process chemicals, and application of stringent quality control principles, Digital minimizes the amount of waste generated during the manufacturing stages. One example of success in this area is the elimination of Class I ozone depleting substances (ODS). Digital's record of eliminating ozone depleting substances from its manufacturing processes well in advance of mandated deadlines was publicly recognized.

Energy Efficiency

The US EPA estimates that customers can save an average of $58 per year in energy costs for each Energy Star compliant personal computer. Digital's Commercial Desktop Personal Computers meet or exceed the energy efficiency standards set by various government purchasing policies, including US EPA Energy Star, Sweden's TCO'92, the Nordic Council's White Swan, Germany's Blue Angel, the Swedish National Board for Industrial and Technical Development (NUTEK), and other commonly recognized voluntary energy efficiency programs. In addition, associated video terminals and printers also meet the energy specifications of EPA's Energy Star program. The VT 525, VTLan 40, and DORIO-VGB, for example, all meet the Energy Star specifications. A series of dot-matrix, ink-jet and laser printers complete the range of Digital products carrying the EPA Energy Star certification.

Studies have demonstrated that a large percentage of computer and office automation users never turn off their equipment because of the inconvenience of rebooting, warm booting, or opening applications. By integrating automatic energy saving features into the Digital Commercial Desktop Personal Computers, customers experience reduced power bills, reduced fan noise, and reduced demand on the building's air conditioning systems, while reducing air pollution from power generation.

Leadership in Energy Efficiency

In 1992, Digital Equipment Corporation joined in partnership with the United States Environmental Protection Agency (EPA) to support the EPA's newly created Energy Star Program. Digital committed itself to develop energy-efficient personal computers that conserve energy, last longer and are less expensive to operate. Digital is also playing an active role in Europe in the development of an international proposal for energy-efficient office technology, in which European countries joined with Japan and the United States to come up with a common worldwide voluntary program.

3. PACKAGING & DOCUMENTATION DESIGN

Distribution Packaging Reduction

Digital's design program for distribution packaging reduction has resulted in total reduction of thousands of tons of packaging waste since 1990. Digital conducts advanced fragility assessments on products to determine the appropriate packaging for each product. Digital scientifically calculates optimal product packaging, and thereby reduces the risk of damaged products while ensuring that packaging is minimized. When reviewing its manufacturing processes, Digital discovered opportunities to minimize waste from packaging used by suppliers delivering components for Digital products. Working together with suppliers, Digital has achieved notable results in reducing components packaging waste. For example, in 1994, due to cooperation with the PWB (Printed Wiring Boards) suppliers, a packaging waste reduction of 68 tons was achieved. Another example: the Digital manufacturing facility in Ontario, Canada, negotiated an arrangement with suppliers to minimize the amount of packaging used for components sent to the plant. Under this arrangement, bulk deliveries from a major supplier of powered enclosures now arrive in returnable and reusable packaging. After unloading the components, the supplier takes the packaging back for reuse.

Recycled Content

In a constant search for conservation of natural resources Digital introduced recycling materials into its packaging. Paper with 10% to 60% recycled content is used for product documentation, and the corrugated packaging in which the products are presented to the customer contain up to 60% recycled fibers. Cushioning foams for packaging contain up to 15% recycled materials.

Heavy Metal Content

Packaging is designed to meet heavy metal content restrictions imposed by various US states and the European Union. In response, Digital requires that the heavy metal content in packaging materials, including inks used in marking, is reduced to minimal attainable levels. The non-incidental accumulated total for lead, mercury, hexavalent chromium and cadmium may not exceed a concentration of 100 parts per million in any packaging component.

Recyclability

Likewise, Digital ensures that in distribution packaging the use of glue and other adhesives to attach unlike materials is minimized. Using glue to attach foam and corrugated fiberboard in packaging results in reduced recyclability of packaging materials. Avoiding the use of glue to attach corrugated paper and foam allows both the foam and the corrugated paper to be separated and recycled. Also, all corrugated fiberboard packaging is made from unbleached, natural fiber materials. In addition to the simplification of sorting and recycling, packaging materials such as plastic foams and wraps are clearly marked with internationally recognized material identification codes to identify the specific material composition.

4. PRODUCT TAKE BACK

Governments and customers are increasingly looking for suppliers to take responsibility for products after they have served their intended use. In fact, Digital is implementing a process for product take-back in anticipation of the European Union and individual country requirements. Digital was a pioneer in product take-back in the late-1980s and now offers a complete product disposition and recycling service for computers and other related products.

Digital currently operates Recovery Centers in the United States (Contoocook, New Hampshire) and in Europe (Nijmegen, Netherlands). Owned and managed by Digital, these organizations control product recovery and material recycling using processes that are both economical and protective for the environment. The process is as follows : incoming computer equipment received at the Recovery Centers is inspected. Valuable equipment is sold for reuse, repaired or refurbished. Generic components (integrated circuits and memory chips) with a commercial value are also extracted and sold to second hand component vendors for reuse. The remaining equipment is then dismantled and separated into several fractions of materials. These groups of materials are then dispatched to specialized vendors for recycling or disposal under controlled and Digital-qualified processes. The de-manufacturing, disassembly, and disposition processes are carefully controlled to protect the environment as well as the health and safety of the employees and local communities.

5. CONCLUSION

Digital has a long tradition of achievement in environmental health and safety. Today as the company moves forward and faces new challenges, managers recognize that Environmental, Health & Safety issues are an integral part of our business.

Digital believes the most effective, efficient method of ensuring Environmental, Health & Safety sound management, is to integrate it so deeply within each business function and operation that it is indistinguishable from any other business activity. In so doing, businesses will realize that it is a critical mission component which will provide them with new opportunities while achieving sustainable development , growth and profitability.

CHAPTER 10

DETERMINANTS OF THE LIFE SPAN OF HOUSEHOLD EQUIPMENT:
The Case of Poland

MICHEL KOSTECKI
University of Neuchâtel

WIKTOR KISIEL AND EWA BOGACKA-KISIEL
University of Wroclaw and The Academy of Economics in Wroclaw

What are the determinants of the life span of household equipment? This study focuses, in particular, on a relationship between the durability of household equipment and the following variables:

1. the relative price of repair services (in comparison with the prices of new equipment);
2. change in consumer purchasing power (defined as the average *per capita* income compared to the price of new equipment);
3. changes in consumption patterns (e.g. a move away from collective to individual consumption, demand for imported equipment and a shift in purchasing power);
4. price ratio of new equipment and energy.

Poland's economy of the nineties provides a particularly suitable context for such an examination:

- during the transition period initiated in 1989, the country's price system was drastically modified;
- the foreign trade regime has been decentralized and Poland's import controls have been liberalized to allow more foreign competition;
- the purchasing power of numerous segments of the population increased in the mid-nineties as compared to the pre-transformation period; and
- consumption patterns have undergone a profound change.

Hence, Poland's market for household equipment and its maintenance services during the 1989-1996 period may be regarded as a laboratory situation in which the relationship between the life span of consumer durables and a number of its determinant variables can be analyzed.

M. Kostecki (ed.) The Durable Use of Consumer Products, 105–112.

Our research is based on in-depth case studies of Polar – Poland's market leader in washing machines and refrigerators – as well as of BIOFROST Co. – a Wroclaw service firm conducting repair works. The studies involved interviews with managers, repairmen, and salesmen, as well as a series of twenty face-to-face interviews with the products' users.

Both companies are located in Wroclaw, Silesia, a region situated in the south-western part of the country close to the Polish-German border. Wroclaw has a population of some 700 000 and is one of the most important Polish economic centers. Established in the early seventies, Polar acquired a quasi-monopolist position in Poland's market for refrigerators and washing machines in the eighties. With the annual production of some 260 000 washing machines and over 400 000 refrigerators and freezers, Polar's supplies accounted for almost 50 per cent of the country's market share in the mid-nineties.

Table 10.1

NUMBER OF REFRIGERATORS AND WASHING MACHINES PER 100 HOUSEHOLDS IN POLAND (1991-95)			
Year	1991	1993	1995
Washing machines	43	64	62.2
Refrigerators	94	98	100

Source: Polityka, No 1 (1996) and Polar's estimates.

In 1995, twelve million Polish households were almost entirely equipped with refrigerators and over half of them had washing machines. Table 10.1 shows the percentage of households equipped with such appliances and indicates that the use of washing machines and refrigerators has substantially increased during the period of economic transformation. Virtually every household in Poland was equipped with a refrigerator by 1995.

In the eighties, i.e. during the decade preceding the transformation period, the longevity of household equipment in Poland used to be particularly long. For more than half of the equipment, it substantially exceeded the normative technical limit of ten years usually applied to washing machines and refrigerators. The results of a survey conducted in Poland in 1994 are shown in Figure 10.1. The figure presents the breakdown of the household equipment by age for 1994.

A series of investigations done in service stations in the city of Wroclaw, show that the demand for repair services has considerably decreased during the transformation period (1989-1996) showing a distinct jump between 1993 and 1994 (see Figure 10.2).

Figure 10.1. Life Span of Washing Machines and Refrigerators in Poland (1994)

Washing machines

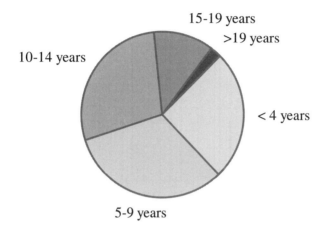

Refrigerators

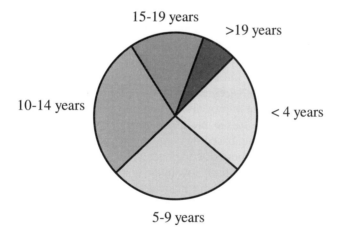

Source: R. Nowacki: *Marketing i Rynek*, No 12 (1995)

Figure 10.2. Changes in Number of Repairs by Service Station (Percentages, 1989 = 100)

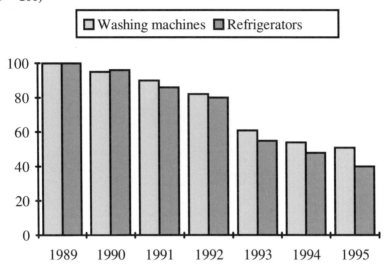

Source: BIOFROST Co.; the data refers to the city of Wroclaw.

It is revealing to observe that the decrease in demand for repair services took place against the background of a stable price ratio for services and equipment and a substantial growth in the number of household equipment in use. That trend was due to (a) a substantial decrease in the average age of the equipment and (b) improvement in the equipment's reliability. The latter development is a tendency observed in the case of a number of products in the OECD countries. For example, in the case of cars, no later than in 1993, periodic maintenance services were required after every 10 000 km or every six months. Today, the recommended interval for numerous trademarks is 15 000-20 000 km or once every 1-2 years (Bald, 1997). In Poland, the improvements in product reliability were particularly impressive in comparison to the pre-transformation period because of a shift towards the market economy based on competition and open markets, the availability of higher quality (imported) components, turn-around management at the Polar factory itself and a particularly low initial quality of 'socialist' equipment.

The average life span of washing machines and refrigerators in Poland decreased between 1989 and 1996. What were the major forced behind such a rapid replacement of 'old by new' during the years of economic transformation (1990-96)? [1]

---

[1]   Statistical data for this study were collected by Dr. Wiktor Kisiel and Professor Ewa Bogacka-Kisiel. A grant by the Swiss Scientific Research Foundation (FNSRS) enabled Dr. Kisiel's participation in the Fourth International Conference on Marketing Strategies dealing with durable use of products at the University of Neuchâtel, in May 1996.

Figure 10.3. Price Ratio Repair / New Equipment (Poland, 1990-95, percentages)

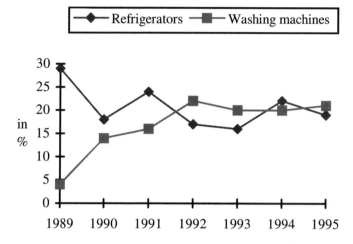

Source: BIOFROST Co.; the data refer to the city of Wroclaw.

Hypothesis 1: An increase in the relative price of repair services reduced the life span of household equipment.
The hypothesis that the trend towards less durability was due to the changes in product / repair service price ratio (see Ch. 1, proposition 6) had to be rejected. Indeed, as shown in Figure 2, the cost of repair services over the price of new equipment did not change much during the period considered and could not have a determinant effect on the substitution between new and old as suggested by Adler and Hlavacek in an earlier study (1976). (Price statistics referring to repair services cover only repairs which required replacement of spare parts and were delivered by BIOFROST Co, a service company in Wroclaw.

Hypothesis 2: Shorter life span of household equipment was induced by the increase in the relative cost of energy.
Though the technical changes introduced in the last years for washing machines did not lead to considerable savings in consumed energy, the opposite is true for refrigerators.

New product lines were successively introduced, with considerably lower energy consumption. Figure 10.4 presents the average monthly cost of energy consumed by an old refrigerator compared with that of the new models. (Note that extremely low operation costs for 1989 were due to the undervalued exchange rate of the Polish zloty). The energy price increases in Poland were substantial. It is not rare in the late nineties that a household spends close to 20 per cent of its disposable income on payments for heating, gas and electricity. The increases in energy prices seems thus to constitute one of the main cost-factors, leading to the substitution of the old equipment by the new models. This message has been used by Polar in its publicity campaign to promote refrigerators sales. The second hypothesis is thus confirmed for the case of refrigerators.

Figure 10.4. Monthly Energy Cost: Old and New Refrigerators Compared (1989-1996) (US dollars)

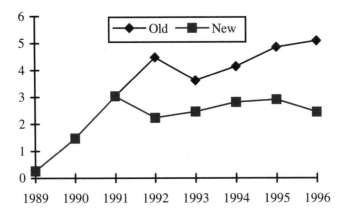

Hypothesis 3: A shorter life span of household equipment was encouraged by the increase in purchasing power of major market segments in Poland.
The prices of new refrigerators and washing machines expressed in terms of the average monthly salary decreased over the 1989-96 period, indicating higher purchase power of major consumer groups in Poland (Figure 10.5).

Figure 10.5. Price of New Equipment Expressed As the Number of Average Monthly Salaries

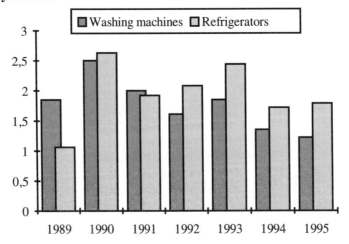

The response to the increases in the purchasing power was further reinforced by the fact that the transformation processed meant an end of the shortage economy (Kornai, 1980). Household equipment is now easily available in shops and the product range is similar to that offered in advanced markets. Easier availability of new products and a wider range of offered trademarks contrast with the waiting lists in shops only a few years ago.

Moreover, the substitution of old by new has an important symbolic dimension, especially for the higher income consumer population (the country's rising *bourgeoisie*). Polish households aspiring to a new life style and economic success exhibit the usual need for expressing their achievement in the material language of symbolic consumption (a 'kitchen demonstration effect'). Publicity is without doubt an important factor which contributes to increasing the demand for symbolic attributes of household appliances.

Since the early nineties the consumer population in Poland was treated to a new form of regular and intensive commercial indoctrination (Kostecki, 1996). Transition economies offer a particularly fascinating case for scientific research on the impact of publicity on values and consumption patterns.

Hypothesis 4: Demand for new household equipment is encouraged by high technical obsolescence of the equipment already in use.
The extension of a product's longevity is not always a good solution for technically obsolete products, the lives of which have been already over-extended. A series of interviews with the products users permitted identification of a number of critical incidents which resulted in the elimination of the equipment:
- security concerns (especially in the case of washing machines);
- unsatisfactory technical performance of old equipment (e.g. noise and poor cooling for refrigerators and destruction of cloth and leakage in the case of washing machines);
- incompatibility with environmental norms (e.g. the use of chlorofluorocarbons in the old refrigerators which is currently illegal);
- no spare parts available for old equipment from the Soviet Union, GDR or the Czech Republic;
- lack of certain functions (e.g. no-frost for refrigerators or special programs for delicate fabrics or wool for washing machines).

All of the above points support the hypothesis that particularly high levels of technical obsolescence in the last years of the communist economy required a rapid renewal of household equipment.

Moreover the old 'socialist' appliances, even when repaired, still provide a considerable risk of malfunctioning, health hazard or worse performance. Therefore, the observed tendency to shorten the useful life of these products seems to lead to their optimal use, minimizing at the same time the negative environmental effects.

Hypothesis 5: Shifts in the consumption patterns considerably accelerated the elimination of old refrigerators and washing machines.
Among the argument quoted by the equipment users, the following seem particularly relevant:

- There was a drastic change in household needs resulting from the improvement in retailing and large availability of food. During the communist years, the population used to stock food from fear that certain products would not be available the next day;
- Poland's economic transformation has radically altered the way many people live. Segments of the population have drastically modified their standard of living and replaced old household equipment by new and more performing equipment;
- New preferences concerning types and sizes of equipment also resulted from demographic changes which additionally reinforced the purchasing power effect (e.g. older people prefer smaller refrigerators while young families often choose large ones with a separate freezer compartment).

The cost of getting rid of the old household equipment after use is of very little importance in Poland, since consumers are not charged when they dispose of old units.

It may be thus concluded that the considerable reduction in the life span of household equipment during the economic transformation process in Poland was due to:

- the necessity to replace the obsolete and ill-performing equipment in use which constituted a health hazard and an environmental threat;
- the increasing cost of use of old models resulting from rapid increases in energy prices (especially in the case of refrigerators);
- the improved purchasing power of large segments of the population and rapid changes in consumption patterns of Polish consumers.

It seems that in the case considered, the lowering of the life span of household equipment represented a move to a more optimal product use both from the consumer's and the environment's perspective.

BIBLIOGRAPHY

ADLER, L. and HLAVACEK, J. (1976) The Relationship between Price and Repair Service for Consumer Durables, *Journal of Marketing*, vol. 40, pp. 80 -82.

BALD, TOBIAS (1997) *La Fidélisation de la clientèle dans le commerce des automobiles: l'example de SMART – un joint venture Mercedes-Benz et SMH*, Mémoire de licence en marketing, Institut de l'Entreprise, Université de Neuchâtel, 1997 .

KORNAI, J. (1980) *Economics of Shortage*, Amsterdam, North Holland.

KOSTECKI, MICHEL (1996) 'Business Options in the Service Sector of the Transition Economies: A Framework for Inquiry' in *Services in the Transition Economies: Business Options for Trade and Investment*, Oxford, Pergamon Press, pp. 3-28.

CHAPTER 11

COLLECTOR'S CAR AND MARKETING OF NEW VEHICLES:
The Case of Daimler-Benz AG

MAARTEN DE GROOT AND BRYN MCCROSSAN MAIRE

University of Neuchâtel

Corporate strategies concerning collectibles offer interesting experience lessons for other areas of consumer durables with important symbolic content. Indeed, numerous car manufacturers with long histories in the automotive industry, utilize their early models as a means of reinforcing their image, increasing their client loyalty and contributing to the prestige of the brand name. This case study deals with the corporate strategy of the leading German car manufacturer, DAIMLER-BENZ AG, concerning services around the older Mercedes models, as well as the related marketing opportunities. It is shown that reconditioning of collector car models both provides a profitable business opportunity and reinforces the company's image of quality producer, which is important in marketing of new vehicles.

MERCEDES – THE IMAGE OF DURABLE QUALITY PRODUCTS.

The first Mercedes car was produced in 1886. Over more than a century of activity, the company has acquired the reputation of being a particularly reliable manufacturer offering solid but technically advanced products. The average life span of numerous Mercedes models has exceeded that of most other vehicles.

Durability is an integral of the Mercedes-Benz's philosophy. This can be seen at several levels and is frequently exploited in the Daimler-Benz's promotional material. For example, the launching of the E-class estate refers to symbolic attributes of durability. The company's publicity material states: "Like its best selling predecessor, the E-class estate embodies all traditional values of Mercedes cars in a stylish functional form ... so it will remain elegant for many years to come" (Daimler-Benz, 1997d). However, durability is not only stressed at the symbolic level, it is also stressed on the technical and functional level: "There

113

have been two themes running through all Mercedes cars since the earliest days – quality and safety. The sheer number of Mercedes cars still running around our roads after they were built is a testament to their quality" (Daimler-Benz, 1997d). Similarly, durability can be found at the concept level. With regards to the Mercedes-Benz SL: "It was back in 1954 that our American importer, Max Hoffmann, prevented the 300 SL, the famous Gullwing Mercedes, from becoming a nine-day wonder. He persuaded us to create a road-going version, so started the SL legend. ... The spirit of those early SLs lives on in the current model" (Daimler-Benz, 1997e).

There is statistical evidence for Germany demonstrating that Mercedes-Benz cars last considerably longer than most other vehicles. Accordingly, the share of Mercedes-Benz increases with age. For example, Mercedes-Benz cars constitute 15 percent of the total German car stock for cars of one year of age; the corresponding proportion for Mercedes-Benz cars of five years of age increases to 17 percent, and for cars of twenty years and more, the share of Mercedes-Benz cars reaches 58 percent (OTC, 1995b). These data can be used to reinforce the image that Mercedes-Benz cars have high durability. "The older the vehicles, the higher the share of the Mercedes-Benz cars in the corresponding age group" (OTC, 1995b).

The Mercedes-Benz cars are also perceived by the consumers as being particularly durable. In a survey on vehicles that had an engine of at least 1.7 liters and were over 20 years of age, more than 60 percent of respondents cited Mercedes-Benz as the brand that was the most reliable. (OTC, 1995a).

Similarly, the art of uniting tradition and innovation is also a part of the Mercedes-Benz philosophy. Daimler-Benz AG demonstrates an longstanding interest in quality and security which enhances the durability of the vehicle. The marketers make use of that attribute in their communications as illustrated by the following text referring to the E-class estates: "The current E-class estates, like the pioneering Mercedes estates of the mid 1970's, embody all traditions that have made Mercedes-Benz a leader among cars. ... Among (its) many revolutionary developments are the crumple zone and the safety steering system. Daimler Benz was also at the forefront of the development of anti-lock braking systems for cars ..." (Daimler-Benz, 1997d). This combination of tradition and innovation is highly valued by the consumers of the brand. According to a survey published in 1994, Mercedes-Benz was ranked at 76 percent for preserving its traditional values (OTC, 1995a).

2. THE MERCEDES CLASSIC CENTER

The interest in Germany for collectors' cars has jumped. In 1970, the number of cars which were over twenty years of age (this is the age necessary to receive the distinction of being a "collector's car") was 25,000. Today, this number has increased to over 500,000 and keeps on growing.

The consumer age group which identifies itself as being the most interested in classic cars in Germany is between 14 and 29 years old (this represents about 46 percent of the total population interested in Classic cars). However, the leading age bracket of Mercedes-Benz Classic car owners are collectors between 30 and 49 years. These collectors represent 65 percent of all Mercedes-Benz Classic car owners (OTC, 1995d).

It is in response to the above trends that Daimler-Benz AG decided to get directly involved in servicing its Classic models. It was in May 1993 that Daimler-Benz AG became the first car producer to open a center specializing in collectors' cars in Stuttgart-Fellbach. The objectives were both to meet the needs of enthusiast Mercedes car owners and to be the guardian of the Mercedes tradition. "I see the Classic Center as an ideal way of encouraging the public to develop and maintain an interest in the Mercedes tradition" says Max-Geritt von Pein, head of heritage for Daimler-Benz AG of which the Center is a part. It goes without saying that this action increases the prestige and the value added of the brand. On the Mercedes Classic Center Internet site, the philosophy of the Center is summarized as follows: "To restore old automobiles means to preserve history. To drive classic cars means to enjoy history. The Center of the Mercedes-Benz Classic division can help you to restore, to drive and to enjoy your classic Mercedes". (Daimler-Benz, 1997f).

2.1 The Center's Main Objectives

For Daimler-Benz, the assurance that it will maintain its vehicles in proper working order strengthens the quality image to its clientele. This reinforces the loyalty of its current customers in addition to attracting new customers to the brand. More than 70 percent of Mercedes-Benz owners stay loyal to the brand when buying a new car (Classic Cars, February 1996). Is there a better advertisement than a happy and satisfied customer ? To be able to conserve the cars authenticity (this increases the value of the collectable), it is important to ensure that original spare parts for the Mercedes Classic car collection remain available. Owners of old Mercedes should have no difficulty in finding the replacement parts necessary so that their cars can be in proper working order with the brand name guaranty that the parts sold are of good quality.

2.2 The Services Provided

The Stuttgart-Fellbach Center offers a wide range of services to the Mercedes-Benz Classic car owners.

* *A supply of spare parts:*
  "The main idea at the start was to improve the availability of spare parts for Mercedes-Benz Classic cars and we have been highly successful in doing so" explains Stefan Röhrig, director of the Center. "We have developed a real partnership not just with our customers, but with some 150 suppliers as well". The Center's slogan summarizes the main idea: "You can't get more original than

this" (Daimler-Benz, 1997c). Thus, while always putting the accent on authenticity, a list of some 25,000 approved manufacturers spare parts is offered for collector's cars built onwards 1945. However, customers wanting to order spare parts do not need to travel to the Fellbach Center. They can order them directly from the local Mercedes-Benz dealer, not only in Germany but also in Switzerland and many other countries.

- *Advice:*
A team of experts is available at the Fellbach Center in order to answer the different questions of Mercedes-Benz Classic car owners, potential buyers or other admirers of Mercedes Classic cars. In fact every month, the Center receives about 2,000 inquiries.

- *Archives, documentation:*
To preserve the image of tradition, the Mercedes-Benz Classic Center offers its customers all technical literature needed both to help their Classic cars and to keep them as original as possible. Most publications refer to passenger cars built between 1945 and 1975 but documents on earlier models are available upon request. The archives are updated as soon as a new model range becomes part of the Mercedes-Benz Classic Center program. Moreover, customers also have the opportunity to visit the Daimler-Benz Classic Archives. Visitors can access roughly 7,000 meters of shelving containing 110 years of the company's history. The material in the archives includes designs, photos, correspondence, test reports, and prospectuses (Daimler-Benz, 1997b).

- *Classic car expertise:*
A highly qualified team of experts is available in order to evaluate the technical condition of the cars as well as their appearance. The customers receive a complete and objective evaluation of their vehicles which can be a major factor when negotiating the buying or the selling of Mercedes-Benz Collection cars.

- *Classic car restoration:*
The Restoration Service is available for all Mercedes-Benz vehicles which are more than twenty years old. The originality and highest quality of those Classic cars is guaranteed by Mercedes-Benz. The motors and transmissions are repaired by the Mercedes-Benz production units. Some restoration work is done by outside partners which work in close collaboration with the head of the Center. The service also researches the application of new products such as motor-fuels, and lubricants for the maintenance and repairs of vehicles in order to ensure that the cars remain in good condition for a long time.

- *Car Rental Service:*
The Classic Car Rental Service offers a wide choice of vehicles. It allows those who cannot afford to buy, or to restore, a Mercedes-Benz to realize the dream of driving a Mercedes Classic car. For example, a 300 SE Sedan can be

rented for a day (100 km included) for 600.- DM, or a Roadster 300 SL for 1900.- DM (Revue Automobile, 1997).

* *Classic Car Sales:*
The Center sells restored cars with all the guarantees and documentation usually required by serious car collector's. All Classic cars offered for sale have been inspected and restored by the Center's personnel to meet the Center's strict quality criteria.

3. FUTURE DEVELOPMENTS

Different specialized centers similar to Fellbach are expected to be set up in several countries such as Austria, Japan, Switzerland and the United States. In offering these services, Mercedes-Benz hopes to improve the public relations with their customers, reinforce the image of quality, durability and tradition which is such an important part of the brand. No doubt, Mercedes-Benz is a leader in the "durability" strategy among car producers. It offers an interesting example of how the durability of a company's products may be exploited to reinforce the company's image and how the durability attributes of older models may prove useful in the marketing of new products.

BIBLIOGRAPHY

CLASSIC CARS (1996) « Analysis of Classic Car Owners » Questioning of Oldtimer Owners 1993, reprint in *Classic Cars*, February 1996.

DAIMLER-BENZ AG (1997a) « Daimler-Benz Classic », *Press Information*, September 1997, Corporate Communications, Stuttgart, Daimler-Benz Aktiengesellschaft, 8p.

DAIMLER-BENZ AG (1997b) « The Daimler-Benz Classic Archive », *Press Information*, September 1997, Corporate Communications, Stuttgart, Daimler-Benz Aktiengesellschaft, 5p.

DAIMLER-BENZ AG (1997c) « The Mercedes-Benz Classic Centre », *Press Information*, September 1997, Corporate Communications, Stuttgart, Daimler-Benz Aktiengesellschaft, 3p.

DAIMLER-BENZ AG (1997d) *The Mercedes-Benz E-Class Estates*, Stuttgart, Daimler-Benz Aktiengesellschaft, 57p.

DAIMLER-BENZ AG (1997e) *Intelligent Technology, Beautifully Wrapped. The Mercedes-Benz Passenger Car Range*, Stuttgart, Daimler-Benz Aktiengesellschaft, 29p.

DAIMLER-BENZ AG (1997f) *Mercedes-Benz Classic Car Center,* http://www.mercedes-benz.com/e/mbclassic/center/default.htm.

LECHNER, HERIBERT (1997) » Mercedes-Benz Classic perpétue une sacro-sainte tradition » *Revue Automobile*, no.46, November 6, Berne, Hallwag SA, pp. 13.

OTC (1995) « Average Age of Vehicles in Germany », *OTC*, August, Stuttgart, Mercedes-Benz Classic Centre.

OTC (1995a) « Analysis of Vehicle Population: Passenger Cars 20 years Old and Over »,

OTC, August, Stuttgart, Mercedes-Benz Classic Centre.

OTC (1995b) « Analysis of Vehicle Population, Market Share of Mercedes Benz », *OTC*, August, Stuttgart, Mercedes-Benz Classic Centre.

OTC (1995c) « Analysis of the Target Group Oldtimer-Prospects », Allsenbach Institut Analysis of Commercials 1994, reprint in *OTC*, September, Stuttgart, Mercedes-Benz Classic Centre.

OTC (1995d) « Analysis of the Target Group of Mercedes Benz Classic Car Owners », GfK Oldtimer-analysis for Mercedes-Benz August 1991, reprint in *OTC*, August, Stuttgart, Mercedes-Benz Classic Centre.

OTC (1995e) « Analysis of the Image of the Car Make: the Value of Company History and Tradition », Image Monitor 1994 MD I, reprint in *OTC*, August, Stuttgart, Mercedes-Benz Classic Centre.

CHAPTER 12

CONCLUSIONS

MICHEL KOSTECKI

Director, The Enterprise Institute, University of Neuchâtel

Product durability is usually looked upon as a key component in assessing a product's environmental impact (c.f. Cooper, 1994 and 1996, Börlin and Stahel, 1987). The marketing aspects of product longevity are rarely discussed either by the marketing practitioners or in the scientific literature. It is an important omission since the life span of consumer durables is, first of all, about consumer satisfaction.

Indeed, product durability is a particular case of a broader issue of optimal product use and "intelligent" consumption. Marketing has a critical role to play in determining the life span of consumer durables. Its impact on the life of consumer durables may be both positive and negative depending on the marketing system's role in defining the nature and velocity of the flow of goods. The negative impact of marketing on product use (e.g. planned obsolescence) finds its roots in what is referred to as *marketing hypocrisy*.

There exists an ambiguity in the marketing practice (and theory) concerning the borderline between the interests of the firm and the interest of the firm's clients. In some cases those interests coincide; in others, conflicts of interest exist. It is in dealing with the latter that *marketing hypocrisy* is apparent. *Marketing hypocrisy* may be defined as a firm's strategy aiming to ensure that the consumer interprets the determinant attributes of a product to the advantage of the firm yet to his own disadvantage.

There exist two basic types of client-producer relations: (a) communal relations and (b) commercial relations. Communal relations exist when a party involved in a reciprocal relationship truly cares about the well-being of the other party (e.g. a mother-child relationship). Commercial relations are based on the concept of commercial reciprocity (e.g. the exchange of a good for a payment).

Obviously, commercial reciprocity does not necessarily imply that a firm cannot care about its clients' well-being. Commercial reciprocity signifies that the extent to which the firm cares is determined by the contribution of its strategies to the firm's profits. Over the last decade or so, marketing sciences have contributed

M. Kostecki (ed.) The Durable Use of Consumer Products, 119–129.

to enlarger the scope of "corporate care" by showing that it could mean an improved customer loyalty resulting in turn in higher sales and higher profit margins (c.f. Parasuraman, Berry, Zeithaml, 1991, Rust et al., 1994, Keavey, 1996, Karoutchi, Kostecki, 1994).

The sub-optimal use of products is less of a problem in industrial marketing. Organizations, as opposed to individual clients, tend to be more rational. Markets for industrial goods are also characterized by a high buyer-concentration ratio in that few large buyers who do most of the purchasing also have substantial bargaining power. Industrial products are purchased by professionally trained experts, who spend their working lives learning how to evaluate product performance. Optimal use is a critical factor in buying behavior. Sales go to those suppliers who cooperate with the buyers on purchasing requirements such as technical standards, in-time delivery and efficient utilization. Optimal use is one of the key criteria to be satisfied if a sale is to materialize and the business relations are to continue.

Things are different in consumer marketing where buyers (individuals or households) are less "rational" and more responsive to manipulation. Most forces which motivate producers and users to opt for a sub-optimal life span find their *raison d'être* in marketing hypocrisy or are encouraged by it.

There are, however, signs that things are going to change. In high-income countries where too many material goods are chasing too few customers, client orientation is a condition *sine qua non* for business success. Producers who try to expand the size of their market are frequently forced to take market share from competitors. As a result there are winners and losers. The losers are those firms who are unable to innovate and to offer improved products and services to their clients. The winning firms are those who identify new needs, discover opportunities and prove themselves capable of contributing to the values of their customers. It is one of the main propositions of this volume that optimal use is an emerging area in which promising business opportunities arise.

It used to be that manufacturers of consumer durables only made money when they shipped products out. Now a small but growing number of companies is learning how to make money and encourage sustainable consumption by designing durable goods and by taking products back for re-use and re-marketing.

In the mass consumption society, manufacturers of consumer durables designed their products "not to last" in order to ensure a steady demand for their production. When equipment was taken back, it was only to recycle materials with high retail value such as aluminum, steel or copper. But today sustainable product design, retake and re-use is being propelled by new consumer preferences and by legislative proposals aimed at a reduction in waste from consumption. While some companies grouse at the prospect of having to assume responsibility for optimal use of consumer durables, such benefits as competitive advantage through improved consumer loyalty, enhanced image and improved economic returns move others towards optimal use strategies.

In areas such as photographic equipment, the computer or photocopy machine industry, where optimal use is rapidly gaining ground, former "waste" objects now represent marketable assets. As illustrated by case studies in this volume, companies such as Digital, Kodak or Rank Xerox profit a second time by selling refurbished equipment to lower-range market segments and offering remanufactured goods at lower prices than most recent models. Rank Xerox has found the re-marketing of remanufactured photocopy machines highly profitable and imitators are starting to follow suit. Apple, IBM, Hewlett Packard and others put more emphasis on re-marketing and retake (Ottman, 1997).

Frequently, electronic or machine components fetch attractive prices in secondary markets because second-hand products from one area may be well reused elsewhere. For example, numerous companies sell the used obsolete computer components to toy manufacturers who turn them into brains of sophisticated toys and educational aids.

Optimal use and take-back strategies are also important to generate goodwill. Digital was able to improve its image by directing remanufactured computers to charitable institutions and developing countries. Similar initiatives are also becoming popular with other producers of electronic equipment (Care Innovation, 1996).

Optimal use is also gaining ground due to a number of trends which are likely to become more important over the years to come:

- The modern economy is about the quality of life and performance rather than material output and growth. This implies more emphasis on product use and less on growth and quantitative consumption.
- Consumers are more and more concerned with optimal use and waste avoidance. They increasingly want to deal with suppliers who can solve their problems in the utilization process and take back the unnecessary goods rather than those who only sell. There is a shift away from a mass consumption society towards an improved degree of user-friendliness of products and sustainable use.
- A growing number of leading businesses are moving away from the simplistic model of pure profit maximization and growth. They do this to acquire more social obligations, and they worry about the excesses in consumption and their products' impact on the natural world (chapters 7, 8 and 9).
- Traditional patterns of thinking about the extent to which businesses should care about the efficiency of consumption have to break down. In a 1996 Swiss survey, consumers rated durability of cars, house equipment, textiles and hi-fi. equipment among the three most important attributes of these products (Stahel, 1996).

Companies that take the above new trends seriously do not only change their products and commercial approaches but also care about the product re-marketing and services around products required for optimal use. In numerous sectors the resulting pressure towards product stewardship is changing the relationship between firms and their customers. Rank Xerox, for instance is now offering to take back its photocopy machines and re-market them in places where they can be of better use (chapter 8). For a growing number of innovative companies re-marketing and product stewardship is a way of developing closer links with their clients. These companies (e.g. Kodak or IBM) see optimal use as a challenge which enables them to improve customer loyalty. Services around products, including "durability services" are gaining importance and successful businesses draw an increasingly important share of their profits from such services.

There are essentially three basic approaches aiming to optimize the durable use of products:

(1) a straightforward approach which signifies that products are made to last;
(2) a traditional approach relying on schemes of extended product use (e.g. maintenance services) and re-use (e.g. traditional second-hand markets);
(3) a future oriented approach implying a global conception and management of optimal use systems; this would include constant up-grading of products based on re-use of spare parts and compatibility of those parts with the largest possible range of systems (standardization) as well as cost reduction through the economies of scale and scope in re-marketing, re-manufacturing and re-use.

It is the latter option which is most suitable for a modern economy aiming at sustainable consumption and client satisfaction.

It is the contention of this volume that:

- The innovative businesses should extend their program of "product stewardship" and "extended product responsibility" beyond the environmental concerns and move to a systematic application of an "optimal use" concept;
- "Optimal use" is likely to become a center piece of future-oriented strategies for consumer durables marketed in high-income countries;
- The "durable use" attributes may provide an effective way of offering differentiation;
- Leadership in durable use provides an attractive strategic option to move towards leadership in markets for consumer durables.

The major business responses required to challenge the phenomenon of the sub-optimal utilization of products are presented in Table 12.1.

- What should be done to optimize the life of durable consumer goods?
- What marketing challenges are confronting businesses in that area (see Table 12.1)?
- What strategies can be recommended for those who explore the innovative approaches of optimal use? It may be useful to summarize the central recommendations which emerge from this volume and could be directed at the managers and policy-makers who face the challenge.

Table 12.1

BUSINESS RESPONSES TO THE CHALLENGE OF LONGER UTILIZATION OF PRODUCTS		
Driving forces of durability	**Potential barriers to increased durability**	**Potential durability strategies**
Consumer demand for more durable products.	Difficulty in getting paid for increased durability.	Provide "durability" services. Guarantee performance of used products. Communicate benefits of durability.
Public awareness of product durability may be manipulated.	Public bias in favour of novelty. Modifying public awareness is a long and costly process.	Use publicity to render durability "in". Seek the image of durability leadership and social responsibility.
Rising cost of recycling and waste handling.	High cost of repair and remanufacturing.	Design products for repair and remanufacturing. Avoid using non-standardized parts where possible.
Legislation: e.g. the Dutch Law Requiring that a certain percentage of drinks is distributed in refillable bottles.	High cost of re-take schemes and difficulties in motivating users.	Develop marketing approaches and techniques to favour re-take and to reduce its cost through users' participation.
Technologies increasing useful life of products.	Incompatibility with the old technologies	Encourage open systems.
Pressure groups in favour of more durable products (e.g. local repairmen, local packaging industry, environmental groups).	Unnecessary complexity of new products may act as a barrier to entry.	Attributes such as simplicity, reliability and durability may constitute an important selling point.
Business opportunities resulting from new trends towards durability (leadership, consulting).	Numerous distortions (e.g. cheap energy in production, heavy taxes and charges on labor) and "old style" legislation discourage durability.	Lobbying in favour of durability and optimal system performance.

Recommendations for managers:
- Audit your company for profit opportunities resulting from optimal use strategies (Annex 1).
- Seek the image of social responsibility through leadership in optimal use.
- Design products in a manner that optimizes both production and product use.
- Encourage open systems and design products for repair. Ensure compatibility with other products and where possible with new technologies.
- Product attributes such as simplicity, durability and reliability may constitute a source of important competitive advantages. Learn to benefit from them.
- Develop innovative techniques and marketing approaches to encourage retake and reduce the cost of re-marketing through greater consumer involvement.
- Communicate benefits of durable use of your products. Provide reasonably priced durability services and, where perceived risks exceed real risks, offer generous guarantees.
- Contribute to render durability "in" through your communication and appropriate coordination of the communication strategies with other leaders.
- Lobby in favor of optimal product use and against marketing hypocrisy. In your lobbying strategies underline that such an approach contributes to social welfare.

Recommendations for policy-makers:
- There is little doubt that the willingness of companies to practice an optimal use approach is also driven by the regulatory framework set by governments. The following recommendations for policy-makers might create sufficient costs to make wasting expensive, so that optimal use is in the company's self-interest.
- Make price systems work for product durability. Tax pollution and waste and eliminate distorting subsidies (e.g. favoring energy use as compared to labor).
- Extend the producer's responsibility for a product's environmental impact over its entire life cycle.
- Favor certification of product durability and optimal life as an element of eco-labeling.
- Modify legislation limiting use of products (e.g. restrictive definitions of "new products" and rigid replacement requirements which are not justified by eco-efficiency).
- Encourage optimal use through appropriate consumer motivation schemes (e.g. mailing packages back to the manufacturer), re-marketing and communication.
- Ensure competitive pricing and quality of maintenance services through the liberalization of their trade and related investments, as well as the removal of entry barriers, the standardization of components and the limitations on the use of cartel-like arrangements in distribution of spare parts and repair services .

BIBLIOGRAPHY

Care Innovation (1996) Eco-efficient Concepts for the Electronics Industry towards Sustainability, International Symposium & Brokerage Event, Frankfurt, November 18 – 20th, 1996.

KEANVEY, SUSAN (1996) Consumer Switching Behaviour in Service Industries: An Exploratory Study, Journal of Marketing, vol. 59, April 1995, pp. 71 – 82.

KAROUTCHI, JAMIN, KOSTECKI, MICHEL (1994) Customer Orientation in Business Services, European Management Journal, vol. 12, no. 2, pp. 179 – 188.

KAY, JOHN (1995) Foundations of Corporate Success, Oxford, Oxford University Press.

OTTMAN, JACQUELYN (1977) 'Product Take-back is a New Marketing Tool' Marketing News, January, p. 8.

PARASURAMAN, A., BERRY, LEONARD, ZEITHAML, VALERIE (1991) "Understanding Customer Expectations of Service" Sloan Management Review, Spring, pp. 39- 48.

RUST, ROLAND, ZAHORIK, ANTHONY J. AND KEININGHAM, TIMOTHY (1994) Return on Quality: Measuring the Financial Impact of Your Company's Quest for Quality, Chicago, Probs Publishing Co.

ANNEX 1   DO YOU BENEFIT FROM THE CURRENT TREND TOWARDS OPTIMAL
USE OF PRODUCTS?

This short check of your company's attitude and performance in the area of useful life of durable consumer products is intended to provide a benchmark from which you can identify your CURRENT position and assess profitable opportunities.

Directions
Read the following text and consider if, in relation to your firm's current practices, you agree or disagree with each statement made. Evaluate whether your firm is making the most from the current trend towards optimal product durability as compared to the leaders in the area. Calculate your score rating the answers as follows:

$$-3 \quad -2 \quad -1 \quad 0 \quad +1 \quad +2 \quad +3$$
Disagree ❏ ❏ ❏ ❏ ❏ ❏ ❏ Agree

1. Product design and use
Our products and services around them are designed and operated to optimize the products' useful life. Instead of offering products and services, we tend to offer performing systems which fully integrate the issue of optimal use, retake, re-manufacturing, re-marketing and reuse. Our products' design is free of the anti-durability bias which results in production of non-lasting products with the aim of not saturating the market.

$$-3 \quad -2 \quad -1 \quad 0 \quad +1 \quad +2 \quad +3$$
Disagree ❏ ❏ ❏ ❏ ❏ ❏ ❏ Agree

2. Packaging
In packaging products for transportation or sale, we seek to reuse the packaging material. Our packaging design takes into account the requirements of re-take, re-use and re-marketing. Our distribution system is operated to encourage our clients to channel used packaging towards our retake chain.

$$-3 \quad -2 \quad -1 \quad 0 \quad +1 \quad +2 \quad +3$$
Disagree ❏ ❏ ❏ ❏ ❏ ❏ ❏ Agree

3. Guarantee
We are willing to guarantee the durability of our products and to offer performance guarantees for services around them.

$$-3 \quad -2 \quad -1 \quad 0 \quad +1 \quad +2 \quad +3$$
Disagree ❏ ❏ ❏ ❏ ❏ ❏ ❏ Agree

4. Technology

We make use of the best available technology to optimize the useful life of our products. Technological complexity is offered only if it contributes to the user's value chain. We regularly review developments in technology and assess their impact on product durability to identify possible improvements to our product design. While introducing new technology, we attempt to minimize the user's problems of technological incompatibility.

-3 -2 -1 0 +1 +2 +3

Disagree ❏ ❏ ❏ ❏ ❏ ❏ ❏ Agree

5. Consumer preferences

We monitor consumer preferences with respect to product durability and provide the necessary services to assist the consumers in the optimal use of their durables . We also take steps to monitor cost of durable product use from the client's perspective. Client-orientation, for us, signifies a user-oriented durability concept.

-3 -2 -1 0 +1 +2 +3

Disagree ❏ ❏ ❏ ❏ ❏ ❏ ❏ Agree

6. Publicity

We include in our publicity, messages emphasizing the durability benefits of our products. Such a communication strategy reinforces our image of a socially responsible company that cares about the planet and attempts to limit pollution resulting from the production and use of its products.

-3 -2 -1 0 +1 +2 +3

Disagree ❏ ❏ ❏ ❏ ❏ ❏ ❏ Agree

7. Market pressure

We use the environmental factors that influence the market pressures relating to the useful life of products to our advantage.

-3 -2 -1 0 +1 +2 +3

Disagree ❏ ❏ ❏ ❏ ❏ ❏ ❏ Agree

8. Public relations

It is our public relations policy to communicate our performance in the field of product durability as well as the related innovations and concerns to interest groups such as customers, suppliers, shareholders, environmental groups, groups favoring moderate consumption, consumer associations, regulators, governments and the general public.

-3 -2 -1 0 +1 +2 +3

Disagree ❏ ❏ ❏ ❏ ❏ ❏ ❏ Agree

9. Local community

Product durability requires services, re-take, re-manufacturing, re-marketing and re-installation (durability services). Such activities are likely to be performed locally rather than globally. We inform local communities of the potential benefits of more durable products. We consult with them on new developments of durability services and attempt to gain their support for our durable product strategies.

-3 –2 –1   0   +1 +2 +3

Disagree ❑ ❑ ❑ ❑ ❑ ❑ ❑ Agree

10. Legal compliance

We are aware of all current legal environmental standards influencing our products and their use and maintain a dialogue with regulatory authorities. We monitor and tend to influence future standards of product durability. Assisting other companies in upgrading their performance to assure legal compliance is perceived as a possible source of revenue for our company.

-3 –2 –1   0   +1 +2 +3

Disagree ❑ ❑ ❑ ❑ ❑ ❑ ❑ Agree

11. Corporate strategy in the area of useful life of products

We have identified our performance objective in the area of the durability of our products and have clear recommendations concerning the implications of that strategy for product design, customer service, distribution, product re-take, remanufacturing and re-marketing, communication, etc.. Our company recognizes the strategic, environmental and commercial implications to our business of adopting the policy of optimal durability for our products.

-3 –2 –1   0   +1 +2 +3

Disagree ❑ ❑ ❑ ❑ ❑ ❑ ❑ Agree

12. Senior management support

With senior management backing, all segments of our organization are improving our company's performance in the area of product durability in order to increase our firm's profitability and take responsibility for the improvement of environmental performance.

-3 –2 –1   0   +1 +2 +3

Disagree ❑ ❑ ❑ ❑ ❑ ❑ ❑ Agree

13. Employee awareness

Our company encourages awareness among our managers and employees that an improved durability of our products obtained through an adequate product design and durability services offered to our clients may increase profits, contribute to our clients value chain and reduce the negative impact of our production and use of our products on the environment.

-3 –2 –1   0   +1 +2 +3

Disagree ❑ ❑ ❑ ❑ ❑ ❑ ❑ Agree

14. Purchasing policy

We take account of the commercial impact that durability performance of our suppliers can have on our business. We consider the durability impact of using materials and look at the opportunities presented by using alternative, more durable materials where economically sound.

          -3   −2 −1   0 +1 +2 +3

Disagree ❑ ❑ ❑ ❑ ❑ ❑ ❑ Agree

15. Cost management and budgeting

We identify the financial costs associated with producing durable products and services which favor product durability. We also take into account product durability requirements in our areas of budgeting, both short and long term.

          -3   −2 −1   0 +1 +2 +3

Disagree ❑ ❑ ❑ ❑ ❑ ❑ ❑ Agree

GLOSSARY

The lack of precise terminology frequently constitutes a barrier in developing marketing strategies at the firm level. This glossary presents the essential vocabulary used in reference to the optimal use strategies in marketing.

Attributes

Features or characteristics of a product which are important to potential buyers and users. For example, flavor, aroma, caffeine content, price and packaging are attributes of instant coffee. Product durability is also an important attribute of consumer durables. The marketer's task of communicating the durability is a particularly difficult task, due to the intangibility of that attribute.

Client orientation

A marketing strategy which puts the client, his needs and product utilization in the center of the producer's concerns.

Client-oriented strategy

Durable products are offered when desired and not offered when durability is low among the attributes valued by the targeted clients. The firm offers both hardware and services combined in well-performing systems which contribute to the client's value chain and satisfy the firm's business objectives. Product durability is services-based.

Cost-centric strategy

Cost minimization is given priority over durability. Price and availability are main determinants of success in mass consumption societies. There are few services around products. Consumer durables don't last and are expected to be thrown away after a limited use and destroyed or recycled.

Customer's value chain

A series or linked set of actions performed by customer to create value.

Design for Environment (DfE)

DfE designates a practice by which environmental considerations are integrated into product and process engineering design procedures.. DfE practices are meant to develop environmentally compatible products and processes while maintaining product price/performance and quality standards. DfE is conceived to be a comprehensive, multi-disciplinary approach to integrating environmental concerns and constraints into product and process design procedures.

M. Kostecki (ed.) The Durable Use of Consumer Products, 131–135.

Diffusion process

The process by which an innovation enters and gradually assumes importance in an economic system. Factors influencing the speed of diffusion include information technology, competitive pressure and other factors.

Durability

The life span of a product (LP) or durability is the product's actual life in use. It may be different to *the product's economic life* which is determined by the opportunity cost. The product's economic life takes into account the total cost of product utilization in comparison to the cost of using new products. It may be shorter than *the product's technical life* which is determined by the duration of a product's ability to fulfill its technical function.

Eco-design

A product design which aims to minimize the product's overall environmental influence by incorporating environmental criteria related to the whole life-cycle of the product in the development process. Eco-design therefore goes beyond the correction of just one or two negative environmental aspects of a product and considers the product as a whole.

Eco-efficiency

The production and consumption which reduces negative ecological impacts and use of resources throughout the product's life cycle below nature's estimated carrying capacity (based on BCSD, 1993).

Extended Product Responsibility (EPR)

A business strategy aiming at resource conservation and pollution prevention, and similarly to the voluntary stewardship model, also advocates a life-cycle perspective to identify strategic pollution prevention and resource conservation opportunities. The principle of shared responsibility ensures that designers, suppliers, manufacturers, distributors, users, and disposers each take responsibility for the environmental impact of products throughout the entire product life.

Fad

A fashion that arrives quickly, becomes popular and declines very fast. Fads typically don't satisfy a strong need nor do they satisfy it well.

Fashion

A distinctive form of human expression of a basic and lasting nature (style) that is currently popular.

Global product

A product with a universally recognized brand name (e.g. Kodak, Rank Xerox or Digital). The universality of certain human needs and wants is one reason for the rapid expansion of global products, another being the productive and marketing capacities of large multinational corporations.

Globalization

A more advanced and complex form of internationalization, which implies a degree of functional integration between internationally dispersed business activities.

Intensive use

A use pattern which multiplies the occasions of product use. For example, an intensive use of a vacation apartment may be encouraged by a periodic rent or a time-sharing arrangement.

Lake economy

A sustainable economy in which the economic success is de-coupled from resource throughput. A 'lake economy' operates at a higher level of resource productivity than a 'river economy' i.e. it is able to produce the same utilization value out of a greatly reduced resource throughput.

Lead users

Clients with needs that, for the time being, are not prevalent but may be expected to become frequent in the future.

Marketing hypocrisy

A firm's strategy aiming to ensure that the consumer misrepresents the determinant attributes of a product to the advantage of the firm and to his own disadvantage. Marketing hypocrisy remains at the center of the sub-optimal use (Kostecki, ch. 11).

Marketing strategy

A statement indicating where the major efforts of a firm should be directed in order to attain the overall marketing goals. It provides a framework which guides the elaboration of marketing plans and links the firm's objectives with the results achieved through the implementation of the marketing plans. Marketing strategy is a centerpiece for managing any firm that is market oriented.

Meta-product

A product surrounded by services such as durability services (e.g. repair, retake or re-marketing services).

Network

A set of interactions among a number of players who collaborate to gain value from their relationship. Networks comprising producers, users, distributors and marketers are important to ensure optimal use of products.

Optimal use

The use of a product which optimizes three essential dimensions: consumer efficiency, intensive use (i.e. frequent use of a product by a large number of consumers) and durable use, i.e. an optimal life of a product.

Optimal use system (OUS)

A system composed of producers, intermediaries and consumers operating in partnership and aiming at the optimization of both production and use.

Personal product
A product for which the exclusivity of its use is an important determinant of consumer satisfaction.

Planned obsolescence
Products are designed to have uneconomically short lives, with the intention of forcing consumers to repurchase too frequently.

Product-centric strategy
The firm puts most of its energies into making solid, durable hardware. It is assumed that a "good product" should sell by itself. Technical quality rather than client's preferences guide the product design. Services around products, such as repair or installation services are aimed at optimal technical functioning of the supplied product rather than at client satisfaction.

Product life or durability
The product's actual life in use. It may be different to *the product's economic life* which is determined by the opportunity cost. The product's economic life takes into account the total cost of product utilization in comparison to the cost of using new products. It may be shorter than *the product's technical life* which is determined by the duration of the product's ability to fulfill its technical function (ch. 1).

Product stewardship
A concept originally developed at Dow Chemical in the early 1970s. Product Stewardship focuses on making environmental, health and safety concerns a priority in all phases of a product's life-cycle and, as a result, lessens the adverse impact of products on human health and the environment.

River economy
An industrial economy of a linear structure in which success, both at the micro and macro level, is directly coupled with resource flows of both matter and energy (Stahel). Also see: 'Lake economy'.

Sales-oriented strategy
The firm puts most of its energies into hard selling. Given its product concept and production capacity it concentrates on promotion to stimulate more buying. Clients are assumed to resist purchases and have to be coaxed into buying. Producers and distributors stimulate demand by increasing symbolic obsolescence of their products (e.g. by promoting new fashion).

Sustainable consumption
A consumption which improves the quality of life, while minimizing waste, pollution and the use of natural resources, over the product life cycle (BCSD,1995).

UNCED

The United Nations Conference on Environment and Development which has on its agenda sustainable production and consumption. The UN Commission on Sustainable Development (UNCSD), in cooperation with national governments, the OECD, and other international organizations is expected to take a leadership role in the area of sustainable development.

BIBLIOGRAPHY

ADLER, L. and HLAVACEK, J. (1976) 'The Relationship between Price and Repair Service for Consumer Durables', *Journal of Marketing*, vol. 40, pp. 80-82.

AFNOR (1978) 'La durée de vie et la durabilité des biens', *Courrier de la Normalisation*, 260, mars-avril.

AKERLOF, GEORGE (1984) *An Economic Theorist's Book of Tales*, Cambridge, MA, Cambridge University Press.

ANDERSON, W.T. CUNNINGHAM, W.H. (1972) 'The Socially Conscious Consumer', *Journal of Marketing*, vol. 36(4), pp. 23-31.

ASHLEY, S. (1993) 'Designing for the Environment', *Mechanical Engineering*, March, pp. 52-55.

BAILLON, J., CERON, J. P. (1976) *Durabilité des biens et question de l'environnement*, Etude effectuée pour le Ministère de la Qualité de la Vie.

BAUDRILLARD, J. (1970) *La société de consommation*, Paris, Denoël.

BAUDRILLARD, J. (1973) *Le miroir de la production*, Paris, Casterman.

BAUDRILLARD, J. (1976) *L'échange symbolique et la mort*, Paris, Gallimard.

BEBBINGTON, J. GRAY, R. (1992) 'Greener Pricing', *Greener Marketing*, Martin Charter (ed.), Surrey, Greenleaf.

BERGANS, J. and CORNET, J. (1996) 'Sustainable Chemistry', *Industrial Crops and Products*, Oxford, Elsevier (forthcoming).

BERIDOT, CHRISTIAN (1979) 'Durée de vie des biens, rationalité économique et mode de développement', *Consommation*, Credoc.

BIDDLE, DAVID (1993) "Recycling for Profit: The New Green Business Frontier", *Harvard Business Review*, November-December 1993.

BORDENAVE, PH. (1978) *Faut-il allonger la vie des biens durables?*, Etude publiée par la Délégation aux économies de matières premières, Paris .

BÖRLIN, MAX (1994) "Governmental Instruments for a Policy of Waste Prevention at Source", *Low-waste Technology and Environmentally Sound Products*, ENVWA/SEM 6/R.31, UN-ECE, Warsaw.

BÖRLIN, MAX, STAHEL, WALTER R. (1987) "Stratégie économique de la durabilité – éléments d'une valorisation de la durée de vie des produits en tant que contribution à la prévention des déchets", *Cahier SBS*, 32, Novembre.

BÖRLIN, MAX, *Impact on Employment of Strategies for Long-life Products and Product-Life Extension*, Paris, OECD Environment Directorate (confidential).

BÖRLIN, MAX (1993) 'Strategien des Bundes zur Abfallvermeidung in der Schweiz', *Neue Wege ohne Abfall, Tendenzen, Fakten, Strategien*, IfÖR (ed.), Berlin.

BÖRLIN, MAX, STAHEL WALTER R. (1989), *An Economic Strategy of Durability*, Geneva, The Product-Life Institute (memo).

BREWER, JOHN and PORTER, ROY (1993) Introduction, in Consumption and the World of Goods in the 17 th and 18 th Centuries, Brewer, John and Porter, Roy (eds.) London, Routledge.

BREWER, JOHN (1995) *Studing Contemporary Consumption: What Can We Learn from*

137

M. Kostecki (ed.) The Durable Use of Consumer Products, 137–142.
© *1998 Kluwer Academic Publishers. Printed in Great Britain.*

the Early Modern Era, Conference Paper, Berlin

BRISTON, J.H. NEILL, T.J. (1972) *Packaging management*, New York, Grower Press.

BULOW, J. (1986) ' An Economic Theory of Planned Obsolescence', *Quarterly Journal of Economics*, pp. 729 – 748.

BURROWS, BRIAN (1993) 'Essay Review- The Greening of Business and Its Relationship to Business Ethics', *Long Range Planning* , vol. 26, no. 1.

CAIRNCROSS, FRANCES (1992) "Recyclage en Europe: l'Allemagne mène la dance", *Harvard l'Expension*, no. 66.

CAIRNCROSS, FRANCES (1994) *Costing the Earth*, London, The Economist Books.

CASEY, E.J. (1992) 'A Plan For Environmental Packaging', *Journal of Business Strategy*, Vol. 13(4), pp. 18-20.

CHICK, A. (1991) 'Greener Packaging', *Greener Marketing*, Charter, M. (ed.), Greenleaf .

CLIFTON, R. BUSS, N. (1992) 'Greener Communications', *Greener Marketing* Charter, M. (ed.), Surrey, Greenleaf.

Commissariat Général du Plan (1975) *Les voies nouvelles pour la croissance*, Paris, Hachette, coll. 'Vivre demain'.

COOPER, TIM (1994) "The Durability of Consumer Durables", *Business Strategy and the Environment*, vol. 3, no. 1, pp. 23 – 28.

COOPER, TIM (1996) *Poor People, Poor Products*, Paper presented at the XIVth International Home Economics and Consumer Studies Research Conference, Roehampton Institute, September, 15 p.

COOPER, TIM (1994) *Beyond Recycling: The Longer Life Option*, November, London, The New Economics Foundation. 21 p.

COOPER, TIM (1994) 'The Durability of Consumer Durables', *Business Strategy and the Environment,* Vol. 1(4), pp. 23-30.

COASE, R. (1972) 'Durability and Monopoly', *Journal of Law and Economics*, no. 15, pp. 143-149.

DALY, H. (1990) 'Towards Some Operational Principles of Sustainable Development', *Ecological Economics*, 2, pp1-6.

DAVIS, J. (1991) *Greening Business: Managing for Sustainable Development*, Basil Backwell.

DECHANT, KATHLEEN, ALTMAN, BARBARA (1994) 'Environmental Leadership: From Compliance to Competitive Advantage", *Academy of Management Executive*, vol. 8, no.3.

DEUTSCH, CHRISTIAN (1994) *Abschied vom Wegwerfprinzip – Die Wende zur Langlebigkeit in der industriellen Produktion*, Schäffer-Poeschel.

DI GENNARO, MONICA and VENTIMIGLIA, PATRIZIA (1996) *La durabilité dans l'emballage, mémoire de licence en marketing,* Université de Neuchâtel

DOWNES, A. (1972) 'Up and Down With Ecology – the Issue Attention Life-cycle', *Public Interest*, 28, pp. 38-50.

DUPUY, J. P., GERIN, F. (1975) 'Société industrielle et durabilité des biens de consommation', *Revue Economique*, vol. 16(3).

EEC (1978) 'Influence de la durabilité sur le bilan énergétique. Etudes de cas', *Rapport pour la DG Energie de la Commission des Communautés Européennes*, Paris, CPT/RPA.

ELKINGTON, J. (1994) 'Toward the Sustainable Corporation: Win-Win-Win Business Strategies for Sustainable Development', *California Management Review*, Vol. 36(2), pp. 90-100.

VAN ENGELSHOVEN, JEAN MARIE HUBERT (1991) *Long Range Planning* vol. 24, no. 6.

ERVINE, W. C. H. (1984) "Durability, Consumers and the Sale of Goods Act", *Juridicial Review*, pp. 147-162.

FALKMAN, E.(1995) *Sustainable Production and Consumption – a Business Perspective*, Conches, World Business Council for Sustainable Development Publications.

FISHMAN, ARTHUR, GANDAL, NEIL , SHY, OZ (1993) "Planned Obsolescence as an Engine of Technological Progress", *Journal of Industrial Economics*, December ,vol. XLI, no.4, pp. 361-370.

FOUQUET, A. (1975) 'La durée d'utilisation des biens durables ménagers évolue peu depuis vingt ans', *Economie et Statistique*, No 72.

FROSCH, ROBERT (1994) 'Industrial Ecology: Minimizing the Impact of Industrial Waste', *Physics Today*, November.

GIRARDBILLE, PATRICIA (1995) *La durée de vie des produits: une analyse marketing*, mémoire de licence en marketing, Université de Neuchâtel.

GIRARDBILLE, PATRICIA and KOSTECKI, MICHEL (1995) Stratégies marketing et durabilité des produits: cas et applications, *Cahiers de recherche en marketing & managegement*, CR-MM-96-02. Université de Neuchâtel.

GRANDI, MICHELA and UDRIOT, FLORENCE (1996) *Le marketing et la durabilité des produits: le cas des vêtements*, mémoire de licence, Université de Neuchâtel.

GALBRAITH, J. K. (1961) *L'ère de l'opulence*, Paris, Calman-Lévy.

GIARINI, ORIO, STAHEL, WALTER R. (1993) *The Limits to Certainty, Facing Risks in the New Service Economy*, Boston, Kluwer Academic Publishers.

GIARINI, ORIO (1994) 'The Service Economy: Challenges and Opportunities for Business Firms', *Marketing Strategies for Services*, M. Kostecki (ed.), Oxford, Pergamon Press, pp. 23-40.

GLAUDE, M. (1977) 'Bientôt 20 millions d'automobiles', *Economie et Statistique*, No. 95.

GLAUDE, M. (1978) 'La fin des vieilles voitures', *Economie et Statistique*, 99.

GRUZON, C. (1974) 'La lutte contre le gaspillage, une nouvelle politique économique, une nouvelle politique de l'environnement', *La documentation française*.

HEITZEL, P (1995) 'Le rôle de la mode et du design dans la société de consommation postmoderne: quels enjeux pour les entreprises ?', *Revue Française du Marketing*, no. 151

HUTCHINSON, COLIN (1992) 'Corporate Strategy and the Environment', *Long Range Planning*, vol. 25, no. 4.

JEANRENAUD, C. SCHWAB, N., SOGUEL, N. (1996) 'Un système de certificats pour la gestion du matériel informatique usagé", *Conception d'un système de certificats échangeables pour la Suisse: analyse de quelques cas pratiques,* Neuchâtel, Université de Neuchâtel (manuscript).

KAROUTCHI, JAMIN, KOSTECKI, MICHEL (1994) Consumer Orientation in Business Services, European Management Journal, vol. 12, no. 2, pp. 179 – 188.

KLEINER, ART (1991) ' *What Does It Mean to Be Green', Harvard Business Review,* July-August

KOSTECKI, MICHEL (1994) 'Le marketing dans l'économie de service', *Revue Française du Marketing*, 149, pp.25-31.

KOSTECKI, MICHEL (1995) 'Product Durability: A Roadmap of Challenges', *Cahier de recherche en marketing & management*, CR-MM-95 -02, Université de Neuchâtel.

KOSTECKI, MICHEL (1996) "Marketing and Durable Use of Consumer Products", *Cahiers de recherche en marketing & management*, CR-MM-96-05, Université de Neuchâtel.

KOTLER, PHILIP (1991) *Marketing Management*, Englewood Cliffs, N.J., Prentice-Hall

KÜRSTEN, W. (1991) 'A Theory of Second-hand Markets: the Rapid Depreciation of Consumer Durables and Product Differentiation Effects', *Journal of Institutional and Theoretical Economics*, vol. 147, pp. 459-476.

LUND, ROBERT T. (1984) 'Integrated Resource Recovery – Re-manufacturing: The Experience of the United States and Implications for Developing Countries', *Joint UNDP / World Bank Report*, Washington DC.

Ministère du Commerce et de l'Artisanat (1975) 'Durée de vie des biens, entretien et réparations', *Rapport ANSQUER*.

MURRAY, FIONA, VIETOR, RICHARD (1994) "Xerox: Design for the Environment", *A Case Study*, Boston, Harvard Business School, N9-794-022.

Network to Reduce Over-consumption: *A Directory of Organizations and Leaders, 1994-95*, Seattle: New Map Foundation.

OTTMAN, J. E. (1992) 'Industry's Response to Green Consumerism', *Journal Business Strategy*, vol. 13(4), pp. 3-7.

OECD (1982) *Product Durability and Product Life Extension: Their Contribution to Solid Waste Management*, Paris

OLSEN, T. (1992) 'Durable Goods Monopoly, Learning by Doing and the Coase Conjecture', *European Economic Review*, no. 36, pp. 157-177.

PACKARD, V. (1962) *L'art du gaspillage*, Paris, Calman-Lévy.

PEARCE, D. (1990) *Report on Sustainable Development*, London, UK Department of Energy.

RUST, ROLAND, ZAHORIK ANTHONY, KEININGHAM TIMOTHY (1997) *Service Marketing*, New York, Harper Collins.

SCHMIDHEIMY, STEPHAN ET AL. (1992), *Changing Course: A Global Business Perspective on Development and the Environment*, Cambridge, Massachussetts, MIT Press.

SCITOVSKY, TIBOR (1994)" Towards a Theory of Second-hand Markets", *Kyklos*, vol. 47, pp. 33-52.

STOKEY, N. (1981) 'Rational Expectations and Durable Goods Pricing', *Bell Journal of Economics*, no. 12, pp. 112 – 128.

STAHEL, WALTER R. (1984) 'Product-life as a Variable: The Notion of Utilization', *Science and Public Policy*, Volume 13 (4), August.

STAHEL, WALTER R. (1988) 'Die Bedeutung der Dauerhaftigkeit von Betriebssytemen (von Computer) für Wirtschaft, Anwender und Umwelt', *Research Report Nr. 502*, Geneva, The Product-Life Institute.

STAHEL, WALTER R. (1993) 'Langlebigkeit der Produkte als Auswag aus den Zielkonflikten beim Recycling?', *Recyclinggerechte Produktentwicklung* -VDI Berichte 1089, Düsseldorf, VDI Verlag.

STAHEL, WALTER R. (1993) 'Life Expectancy of Goods and Future Waste', *International Directory of Solid Waste Management 1993/4* – Copenhagen, The ISWA Yearbook.

Stahel, Walter R. (1993) 'Towards a More Sustainable Society – Implications for After Sale Services', *After Sale Services*, IOCU.

STAHEL, WALTER R. (1993) *Langlebigkeit und Materialrecycling – Strategien zur Vermeidung von Abfällen im Bereich der Produkte,* Essen, Vulkan Verlag.

STAHEL, WALTER R, (1994) 'La stratégie de la durabilité, Une relation nouvelle avec les biens: vendre l'utilisation au lieu du produit', *Entreprendre*, 18, Automne.

STAHEL, WALTER R. (1994) 'Design for Resource Efficiency', *Proceedings of the Design and Ecology Symposium*, Singapore, Goethe Institue.

STAHEL, WALTER R. (1994) 'Eine neue Beziehung zur Verpackung?', *Hüllen füllen – Verpackungsdesign zwischen Bedarf und Verführung*, Schilder Bär, Lotte and Bignens, Christoph (eds), Sulgen, Verlag Niggli AG.

STAHEL, WALTER R. (1994) 'Produkt-Design und Ressourcen-Effizienz' *Herausforderungen für die Informationstechnik*, Zoche, Peter (ed), Heidelberg, Physica-Verlag, Schriftenreihe Technik, Wirtschaft und Politk der FhG-ISI.

STAHEL, WALTER R. (1994) 'Produkt-Design und Ressourcen-Effizienz', *Ethik & Design*, 15. Designwissenschaftiches Kolloquium Burg Giebichen, Hochschule für Kunst und Design, Halle/Saale.

STAHEL, WALTER R (1994) 'The Utilization-Focused Service Economy: Resource Efficiency and Product-Life Extension', *The Greening of Industrial Ecosystems*, Allenby, Braden R. (ed.), Washington DC, National Academy of Engineering, National Academy Press, pp. 178-190.

STAHEL, WALTER R., (1995) 'Handbuch von Beispielen einer höheren Ressourcen Effizienz durch längere bzw, intensivere Nutzung von Güten und Systemen', Umweltministerium Baden-Württemberg, Stuttgart.

STAHEL, WALTER R. (1995) 'Case Studies for Reg 95 on the following companies: Caterpillar, Peoria IL / Corinth MS, USA; DuPont de Nemours (Europe), Geneva; Ecole Hôtelière Lausanne, Lausanne; Geo Insitut Financier, Genève; Hydro Québec, Montréal, Canada', Rencontres Environmentales de Genève 1995, *Proceedings*, GEM 95, Fondation du Devenir, Geneva.

STAHEL, WALTER R. (1995) *Handbuch von Beispielen einer höheren Ressourcen-Effizienz durch längere bzw. intensivere Nutzung von Gütern une Systemen*, Stuttgart, Umweltministerium Baden-Württemberg.

STAHEL, WALTER R.(1995), 'The Impact of Shortening (or Lengthening) the Life-Time of Products and Production Equipment on Industrial Competitiveness and Sustainability', *Research for the DG III of the Commission of the EC*, Brussels.

STAHEL, WALTER R., JACKSON, TIM (ed.) (1993) 'Durability and Optimal Utilization – Product-Life Extension in the Service Economy', *Clean Production Strategies: Developing Preventive Environmental Management in the Industrial Economy* – Stockholm, Environment Institute, Lewis Publishers and Boca Raton, Ann Arbor, London.

STERN, ALISSA (1991) 'The Case of the Environmental Impasse, *Harvard Business Review*, May-June 1991.

VANDERMERWE, SANDRA (1994) 'Service Network Structures for Consumer-Oriented Strategies', *Marketing Strategies for Services*, M. Kostecki (ed.), Oxford, Pergamon Press, pp. 41-64.

VANDERMERWE, SANDRA, ILIFF, MICHAEL D. (1990) "Customers Drive Corporations Green, *Long Range Planning*, vol. 23, no. 6,

VARADARAJAN, P. R. THIRUNARAYANA, P. N. (1990) 'Consumers' Attitudes Towards Marketing Practices, Consumerism and Government Regulations: Cross National Perspectives', *European Journal of Marketing*, Vol. 24(6), pp. 6-23.

VILLENEUVE, A. (1972) *L'équipement des ménages en automobiles (enquête transports 1967)*, Collections de l'I.N.S.E.E, série M 15.

WILLIAMSON, O. (1983) ' Credible Commitments: Using Hostages to Support Exchange' *American Economic Review*, no. 73, pp. 519 – 540.

WILLUMS, JAN-OLAF and GOLÜKE, ULRICH (1992) *From Ideas to Action: Business and Sustainable Development*, A Report Prepared by the International Chamber of Commerce, ICC Publishing and Ad Notam Gyldendal, Oslo.

WOOD, W. (1990) 'The End of The Product Life-cycle', *Journal of Marketing Management*, Vol. 6(2), pp. 145-146.

World Business Council for Sustainable Development (1994) *Eco-efficient Leadership for Improved Economic and Environmental Performance*, Geneva, WBCSD Publications.

World Business Council for Sustainable Development (1995) *Sustainable Production and Consumption: A Business Perspective*, Geneva, WBCSD Publications.

YARANELLA, E. J. LEVINE, R. S. (1992) 'Does Sustainable Development Lead to Sustainability?', *Futures*, Vol. 24(8), pp. 759-774.

PRESS ARTICLES

BRAKE, D. (1993) '486 Processing Power is Wasted on the Average User', *Personal Computer World*, December, pp. 250.

Consumers' Association (1990) 'Green Labeling', *Which?*, January, pp. 10-12.

COY, PETER, NEIL, GROSS (1995) 'The Technology Paradox', *Business Week*, March 6, pp. 36-44.

CRANS ROGER (1994) 'Environnement: Le commerce international perturbé', *Le Monde*, 12-13 June.

CRANS ROGER (1994) 'Environnement: La Suisse recycle ses piles', *Le Monde*, 19 July.

CRANS ROGER (1994) 'Environnement: Le prospère marché de l'antipollution', *Le Monde*, 1 November.

CRANS ROGER (1994) 'Environnement: Le recentrage d'Eco-Emballages', *Le Monde*, 5 April.

DELATTRE LUCAS (1994) 'Un réforme fiscale écologique', *Le Monde*, 15 November.

Fédération Romande des Consommatrices (1995) 'Réparer plutôt que jeter', *J'achète mieux*, 2/95.

HAZAN, PIERRE (1995) 'Des patrons se regroupent pour protéger l'environnement', *Le Nouveau Quotidien*, 4 April.

The Economist (1989) *The Economist Surveys: The Environment*, September

The Economist (1990) *The Economist Surveys: Industry and the Environment*, September

The Economist (1991) *The Economist Surveys: Energy and the Environment*, August

The Economist (1991) "Throwing Things Away", October 5th-11th.

INDEX

M. Kostecki (ed.) The Durable Use of Consumer Products, 143–146.
© 1998 *Kluwer Academic Publishers. Printed in Great Britain.*